BABY COLIC HELP

NATURAL PARENTING SUPPORT

VENETIA MOORE

BABY COLIC HELP

Natural Parenting Support

Published in the UK by
True Nature
Timberscombe
Somerset
TA24 7TD

ISBN. 978-0-9928219-1-3

Copyright © 2014 by Venetia Moore

The right of Venetia Moore to be identified as the author of this book has been asserted by her in accordance with the Copyright, Designs and Patents Act 1988

Book design by The Write Factor

Illustrations by Bea Hammond

Cover photo by Chandra Isenberg
www.chandraisenbergphotography.com

This book is dedicated, with love, to my two sons Luke and Sam, from whom I never stop learning.

A big thank you to everyone who has helped me on my journey of writing this book.

Disclaimer:

The suggestions and treatments described in this book should not replace the care and direct supervision of a trained health-care professional. The recommendations given in this book are intended solely as education and information, and should not be taken as medical advice. The author does not accept any liability for readers who choose to self-prescribe.

"New or old souls being born are our future.
They need to learn of peace, joy and prayer
– so as to get and give the best to life.
To become whole human
beings."

Mata Yogananda Mahasaya Dharma

CONTENTS

INTRODUCTION   1
A book in the making. A new vocation. A holistic approach. Be guided by your intuition. Take heart.

1. WHAT IS BABY COLIC?   7
Signs and symptoms of colic. Identifying the degree of colic and some possible causes. Food Intolerances, sensitivities and common food culprits when breastfeeding. Magic milk (Colostrum). Bottle feeding and formulas. Reflux.

2. WHAT YOU CAN DO FOR YOUR BABY   23
Part One
Baby's Needs Check. Watch the wind – preventing a windy baby. Tips for breast feeding and bottle feeding. Burping. Constant crying. The Power of Touch. Soothing suggestions and techniques. Warm Hands and Colon Circles. Winding down time. Swaddling. Further soothing suggestions.

3. WHAT YOU CAN DO FOR YOUR BABY   37
Part Two
Birth Stress. Some signs and ways to reduce and balance stress levels. Facilitated Crying. Tongue tie. What's your baby saying? Do you use a dummy? The pros and cons. Natural remedies for colic.

4. IN YOUR LOVING HANDS   49
The art of baby massage and the benefits: How to practise baby massage. The baby colic massage routine. Comments from massaging mums and dads.

5. BABY YOGA   65
What is Baby Yoga? Benefits: Some helpful baby yoga exercises. Comments from parents.

6. CRANIOSACRAL THERAPY 73

The craniosacral system. Why might your baby benefit from craniosacral therapy? How does craniosacral therapy work? When is it best for your baby to have a CST treatment? Some comments from parents.

7. WHAT YOU CAN DO FOR YOU 81

You are important. Dealing with emotions. Managing stress. Supplements for mum. Natural remedies. Eating well. Superfoods for mum.

8. BABY BLUES AND POST-NATAL DEPRESSION 95

Information on baby Blues and Post-Natal Depression. Possible symptoms and causes of PND. Suggestions for helping post-natal blues or for when you're feeling low.

9. MORE FOR DADS 105

Different isn't bad just different. You weren't expecting to feel this way. Finding it hard to bond: Feeling down: Jealousy and resentment. Constant crying. Lovemaking changes: Couple care. When advice is given to you on your parenting.

YOU ARE A COLIC HERO! 117

APPENDIX 119
HEART TO HEART WITH YOUR BABY

Heart connection visualisation. Tonglen. A healing light practice.

FURTHER RESOURCES 125

INTRODUCTION

Ideally, having a baby is a joyous experience – but it can also be a very challenging one, especially if your baby has colic. No one can prepare you for the challenges and the impact colic can have on you, your partner and family.

Right now you may be feeling exhausted, disappointed, helpless, disillusioned, worried you are not parenting right, or just plain desperate. If so, you are not alone. It's reported that around 40% of babies in Britain suffer with differing degrees of colic, so there are many parents feeling just the way you do.

The good thing is that there are many ways to help your baby and yourself.

A BOOK IN THE MAKING

My history as a baby colic coach goes back to the mid-1980s, when I had my first child. It was a time when there was very little information available to support and guide parents with a colicky baby. Health visitors did their best to listen and to reassure me that I was doing all that I could, but they knew little about colic so could not offer much in the way of practical help. I became mentally and physically exhausted. My days – and nights – were a constant round of endless pacing and bouncing, and sleep deprivation was taking its toll. Losing my keys, consuming copious amounts of coffee, and leaving the house wearing odd socks (or worse!) all became part of a rather jittery way of life.

Through my fog of sleeplessness, I was constantly trying to rack my brains to come up with something to relieve my son's suffering. However, my first breakthrough didn't come through thinking – and it was set to change both our lives. After yet another disturbed night, and desperate to do something to help, I placed my hands on my distraught baby's body and intuitively started massaging him. Gently but firmly, I massaged his back, legs, feet, hands and tummy. After a short while he began to relax; his crying stopped, and his whole body started to soften. The feeling of empowerment was almost indescribable – at long last, something was working! I was able to help my baby!

Massage became part of our daily routine and we both benefited. It gave him a small window of time without discomfort and it offered me the opportunity to relax and feel peaceful – which benefited both of us. It also began to build a special bond between us.

However, the benefits weren't limited to the actual massage time. Each day there was cumulative progress and, step by small step, my son gradually improved. He slept more deeply and for longer periods; he became less bloated and windy; there were fewer bouts of irritability and fretfulness – and he generally became a happier baby.

Fourteen months later my second son was born and he, too, suffered with colic. However, this time I was better equipped and prepared, and, as a consequence, his colicky phase lasted only half the time of my first son's, and never became so intense.

Massage became part of our daily lives and, as well as benefiting my children, it set me off on a new career path. Since then, I have taught many mums to massage their babies.

I continued to massage both my sons regularly through all their growing years. Massage time was always a special part of the day, a time to give and receive loving energy, and a time to relax together amid our otherwise full lives. It helped to keep the communication between us strong, especially through the teenage years. And having grown-up sons who can now both give me a wonderful massage is indeed a bonus!

Since those first-hand experiences I have always empathized with those facing the colic challenge. I have passionately researched, trained in, and taught different ways to help other parents bring relief to their unhappy babies. I hope my knowledge and experience contained in this book will help you and your baby in many ways.

A NEW VOCATION

My baby colic experiences with my two sons in the 1980s set me on a steep learning curve and steered me towards a new vocation. My discovery of the profound benefits of massage for babies awakened my desire to help others in a therapeutic way, so I decided to add to my initial massage qualification. Essential oils were already playing an integral role in my personal life and I was keen to study more about them. This resulted in my qualifying in 1991 as an Aromatherapist and starting up my own mobile massage business. Then in 1994 I began practising CranioSacral Therapy.

In 1995 I joined a Complementary Health Centre, newly opened in my area by group of forward-thinking doctors. The doctors' influential endorsement was a great asset. My thirst for acquiring more holistic knowledge for improving health and wellbeing continued with further studies of various compatible therapies, leading to my gaining a Clinical Holistic Honours Diploma.

In 1999 I was invited to teach baby massage and baby yoga, so took the necessary training and started running regular baby classes.

Today my studies continue and my practice happily expands. I consider myself very fortunate to have been able to grow and work in such a rewarding vocation – and, in a way, it's all thanks to baby colic!

A HOLISTIC APPROACH

Baby colic is rarely successfully treatable by medication. There is no quick-fix panacea, though there are some alternative remedies that may, in some cases, offer relief of symptoms. This may seem like bad news to many parents but it does offer the opportunity to approach your baby and their symptoms holistically – that is, taking into account all aspects of their being. And, of course, this book is also holistic in the wider sense: it's about helping mums, dads and caregivers – the 'whole' family unit. A baby is best looked after and cared for by adults who look after and care for themselves. The bond between parent and child is more than physical, and your baby is tuned-in to how you are feeling. Looking after you benefits your baby too!

The word 'holistic' means 'considering the complete person,

physically, emotionally, mentally and spiritually.' As such, a truly holistic approach includes more than just treating a set of symptoms with drugs or other treatments. It considers the whole being. Indeed, many mainstream doctors are also recognizing the role that a person's emotional and mental health plays in the creation of physical illness, and vice versa. Dealing with the daily stress of being with a baby suffering with colic can eventually affect your health and well-being.

BE GUIDED BY YOUR INTUITION

Intuition is a sense of clear knowing that comes to you from a place of wisdom deep within. I'm thankful that I heard and acted on my intuition at a time when I felt helpless and lost. It continues to guide and empower me in my life. I believe that we all have this part in us that truly knows what's best; we just need to learn to hear, trust and act on that inner guidance.

You have a powerful connection with your baby, and it's important to acknowledge what you feel intuitively. You may not be able to explain the reason for knowing what you know intuitively but, by tuning in to those feelings, you can become more confident about making your own decisions.

Throughout this book I'll be encouraging you to experiment with trusting and following your inner wisdom – and to see what happens!

TAKE HEART

Although it may seem like an eternity, you can take heart from the fact that colic rarely lasts longer than the first few months of a baby's life. From birth to around four months the immature nervous system and digestive system are adjusting to life in the world outside the womb. Your baby really will grow out of it!

BABY COLIC HELP

CHAPTER ONE
WHAT IS BABY COLIC?

In this chapter, to help you to determine whether your baby has colic, we're going to look at some stages and symptoms of colic. We'll consider some physical and emotional causes, including possible dietary culprits. We'll also look at some breast and bottle feeding suggestions and tips.

Many mums feel that if there's something wrong with their baby, then there must be something wrong with them as the mother. But you must try not to blame yourself; your baby isn't crying because you're a bad parent! In Chapter Eight: WHAT YOU CAN DO FOR YOUR BABY, we'll look more closely at the mixture of natural emotions many people may feel at this challenging time and I'll suggest positive ways to help not just your baby but also yourself – you need some TLC too!

You're likely to receive conflicting advice and information from various sources about how to deal with a colicky baby. You may also hear lots of theories about what colic really is and whether or not your baby has it.

Evidence shows that between 5 – 25% of newborns could show signs of Infantile Colic (Kilgour T, Wade S. Infantile Colic. *Clin Evid 2005*). It's important to remember that, as a parent (even first time around), you possess an innate knowing about when things are 'not OK' with your little one – and, so long as you have checked with a GP or health visitor that there isn't a more serious underlying problem, then your baby can only benefit from the gentle and soothing suggestions contained within this book.

All babies cry on and off and, as your confidence grows, you'll become better able to interpret your baby's different cries and to grasp what your little darling is shouting about! However, this isn't always easy, especially with your first baby. It can feel as though you're having to learn a new language and, until you can achieve that, you have to guess what their needs might be, day and night. Until you get into a natural rhythm with your baby, it's natural to feel a bit overwhelmed from time to time.

Colicky babies tend to cry a lot more than others; those peaceful rest times just don't seem to come often enough. My intention with this book is to offer you some insight into what your baby may be experiencing, and why other soothing techniques may not be working. I'll also be suggesting different ways in which you may be able to help – and reminding you to be gentle with yourself during this challenging time.

It's important to remember that baby colic is self-limiting; the symptoms usually begin subsiding at around the age of four to six months, because, as the digestive system matures, it begins to work more efficiently. This is helped by other developmental changes.

- Internal sleep patterns develop, making for a more relaxed, less stressed baby.
- The baby's sight improves, allowing them to see more clearly across the room, which makes it easier to distract them from any discomfort.
- The baby will be able to suck their own fingers for comfort and play – another good source of distraction!

> ### Are you afraid that you may hurt your baby?
>
> Coping with a colicky baby can be very stressful and it may push you to your limits. It's important to talk to someone urgently if you feel you just can't cope any longer or if you are worried that you are so exhausted and frustrated that, however unthinkable, you might unintentionally shake and hurt your baby.
>
> **Please talk to your Health Visitor or GP!**
>
> There are also helplines and websites, such as www.cry-sis.org.uk, which are especially useful if initially you want to seek advice discreetly.

SIGNS AND SYMPTOMS OF COLIC

Colic affects the stomach and the small and large intestines, causing abdominal pain and discomfort, spasms, inflammation and bloating. The symptoms can vary: see if any of these in the following list might apply to your baby.

Is your baby...

- Being generally restless and fretful and not a happy baby
- Crying frequently and inconsolably, or screaming, with sudden ear-piercing shrieks
- Showing whole body tension
- Drawing the knees up towards the tummy
- Frequently arching the back
- Bloated around the abdominal area most of the time
- Frequently passing wind or straining (often accompanied by a reddened face)
- Not able to establish a good feeding pattern
- Clenching the fists
- Sleeping poorly
- Showing Dr Jekyll and Mr Hyde personality swings?

Or:

- Are you feeling intuitively that something is 'just not right'?

If you have answered 'yes' to most of these questions, it's possible that your baby has colicky symptoms which are causing discomfort somewhere within the digestive system.

> If your baby has a fever (meaning that his or her temperature rises above 39 degrees centigrade) please seek medical advice. Also, if the screaming persists, contact your doctor or emergency services.

IDENTIFYING THE DEGREE OF COLIC

Let's look more closely at the symptoms of colic and their possible causes. In order to help you do this, I have described them in three stages. This doesn't necessarily mean that a baby will move on from one stage to the next; it's simply a way of defining the severity of the symptoms and differentiating between the possible causes.

You'll find ways to help in each stage in Chapter Two: WHAT YOU CAN DO FOR YOUR BABY

STAGE 1 – Early signs of colic (milder symptoms)

WHAT TO LOOK OUT FOR

- Mild moaning and crying, with some mild cramping in the tummy area
- Appearing fretful from time to time
- Having trouble passing wind
- Symptoms often get worse between 6pm – midnight.

SOME POSSIBLE CAUSES

Trapped wind in the stomach can cause pain, discomfort and bloating. Overstimulation or tiredness can cause fretfulness and irritability, especially in the evening. Over-feeding or under-feeding can also cause some of these milder signs.

> ## MYELIN
>
> Myelin is a fatty sheath that covers the nerves. This helps the brain to send messages to the whole body including the stomach and intestines. In babies, myelination naturally takes time to develop; this means that it can take a while for the digestive system to start functioning properly.

STAGE 2 – Intermediate stage (symptoms a little more intense and prolonged)

WHAT TO LOOK OUT FOR

- Crying is becoming more persistent, maybe lasting for an hour or more
- Abdominal pain seems worse and knees are doubling up more frequently
- Colicky symptoms in the day as well as the evening
- Bowel movement is sluggish and often appears uncomfortable.

SOME POSSIBLE CAUSES

At this stage, the discomfort may be around the diaphragm (the elastic sheet of muscle which separates the lungs / chest area from the abdominal area) and in the small and large intestines around and below the belly button. There could be a mixture of reasons for the discomfort, including: trapped wind, diaphragmatic spasms resulting in acid reflux, constipation, tight abdominal muscles and general tension.

STAGE 3 - Persistent stage (symptoms prolonged and intense most of the time)

WHAT TO LOOK OUT FOR:

- Inconsolable crying at any hour of the day or night, often starting after a feed – but really at any time
- Knees constantly being drawn in towards the tummy
- Very difficult to comfort
- You may find that you just cannot establish any routine in any part of the day
- Feeding times are quite a struggle (although some babies can relax a little and find some comfort in suckling)
- Bowel movement is irregular and strained and stools can be either hard or too soft.

SOME POSSIBLE CAUSES

Stage 3 could be related to muscular spasms. In Chapter Six: CRANIOSACRAL THERAPY we'll explore the theory of there being some possible spinal misalignment or impingement on the nerves. This might be due to the position the baby was in during the later stages of pregnancy, the birth experience, or just general tightness and tension in the spine and abdomen.

The Psoas muscles, which flex the hips and bring the legs up towards the chest, may be a little tight. In the latter part of pregnancy your baby has been in a tight ball in the womb; this can shorten the Psoas muscles, which impedes the abdomen from fully expanding to accommodate a feed.

BABY COLIC HELP

> ## THE VAGUS NERVE
>
> *A CONNECTION BETWEEN THE EMOTIONS AND THE DIGESTIVE SYSTEM*
>
> The vagus nerve starts at the brain stem and travels through the neck into the chest and then into the abdomen. It stimulates the lungs and stomach, and the heart-rate and movement in the intestines (peristalsis). Emotions and state of mind are closely linked to the digestive system and this connection is largely due to the vagus nerve. Your baby's emotional wellbeing can affect their digestive system, so calming and comforting techniques do more than just soothe your baby – they also help to settle the tummy.

OTHER POSSIBLE CAUSES FOR COLICKY SYMPTOMS

FOOD INTOLERANCES WHEN BREAST FEEDING

Could what you're eating be affecting your baby's tummy?

Each baby reacts differently to certain foods that the mother has eaten. If your baby is particularly disturbed one day, try to remember what you have eaten in the past twenty-four hours it's possible your baby may be showing signs of a food intolerance. What you eat could be creating intestinal gas; affecting the taste and amount of milk you're producing. If a particular food seems suspect, remove it from your diet for a while and see how your baby responds.

SOME COMMON CULPRITS

- Dairy
- Egg whites (possible allergen)
- Wheat (possible allergen)
- Broccoli, cauliflower, cabbage and Brussels sprouts can cause wind in yourself as well as in your baby
- Onions
- Potatoes
- Peanuts (possible allergen)
- Pulses
- Jerusalem artichokes
- Tea
- Chocolate (possible allergen)
- Spicy foods
- Garlic
- Beans
- Medication (always check with your doctor before taking any medication or stopping prescribed medicines).

ALLERGIC REACTION TO DAIRY PRODUCTS
(Lactose intolerance)

Some research suggests that potentially allergenic beta-lactoglobulin in cows' milk could be transferred to your baby through your breast milk, upsetting the baby's digestive system. Colicky symptoms may start in your baby a few hours after breast feeding, if you have recently eaten dairy products. The baby may be frequently constipated, or have green or mucousy stools. A red allergic ring or rash may

> appear around the baby's anus. Try eliminating dairy products from your diet: if this has been the problem, the baby's symptoms should diminish or stop after a day or two.

Avoid the following as much as possible; they can often cause problems:

- Coffee
- Most artificial sweeteners
- Processed foods (additives, salt and sugar)
- Tuna, because of the mercury content (and limit general consumption of other fish to two average servings a week).

Things to **stop altogether** when pregnant and when caring for a young baby, especially if breastfeeding, are:

- Alcohol
- Smoking
- Recreational drugs.

If you need help to do this, speak to your GP, health visitor or call a helpline.

> ## TEA, COFFEE AND ALCOHOL
>
> Limit the amount of tea and coffee you drink, because the caffeine passing through your milk can make your baby irritable and jittery, and affect your baby's sleep. It's important to limit or stop drinking alcohol as, not only is it harmful to the baby, it's considered not healthy for you; it dehydrates you, and it can also be a depressant. Drinking lots of water will help prevent you from developing maternal constipation, dehydration and blocked milk ducts.

If your baby's symptoms persist, have a chat about it with a health visitor, nutritionist or your doctor. Try joining a local breast-feeding group, where you can share experiences with other mums and get some guidance. The National Childbirth Trust (NCT) and La Leche League will also provide help and guidance.

Remember, with breastfeeding, as with everything else, not all babies are the same and what works for one won't necessarily work for another. Seek advice and try things out and don't despair if one person's solution isn't yours. Experiment for yourself and follow your intuition.

MAGIC MILK (Colostrum)

Colostrum has been called 'magic milk' and 'Nature's vaccine' because it's jam-packed with wonderful health-giving properties. Thicker than breast milk and either yellow or clear in colour, it's naturally available before your breast milk comes in two or three days following the birth.

HEALTH BENEFITS

Colostrum has the very important function of helping to boost your baby's immune system. It's full of the mother's antibodies (immunoglobulins). Proteins, essential factors in immunity, are more concentrated in colostrum than in breast milk.

- Premature babies benefit greatly from colostrum because it contains such a high level of antibodies, helping to prepare and strengthen them ready for an earlier discharge from hospital.
- Colostrum contains other substances, such as oligosaccharides, prebiotics and probiotics, which are good for digestion and are not found in formula milk.
- It's low in fat, which is important as newborns' stomachs are not able to cope with fatty foods.
- It has a mild laxative effect, which helps your baby to pass the first stool.
- There's lots of breastfeeding support available to help you to give your baby this important start with a ready-made magic 'formula'.

BOTTLE FEEDING

Could your formula be causing colicky symptoms? If your baby is bottle-fed with formula and experiencing colic, then it's possible a milk allergy (or intolerance) could be the problem. As far back as 1989 an article in the The Journal of the Royal College of General Practitioners, suggested that infantile colic was resolved in 68% of babies who changed from cow's milk formulas to soya. There are alternatives available and it may be worth discussing these with your health visitor or doctor. There are cows' milk-free or low-allergen lactose free formulas that could make a difference.

GASTRO-OESOPHAGEAL REFLUX (GER)

Excessive hiccups resulting in milk being brought up after a feed (or at other times) is known as reflux, which can sometimes be confused with colic. If your baby is spitting up a lot it could be a sign of reflux. Reflux can be a less obvious cause of apparently colicky symptoms or waking during the night. It occurs when stomach acid regurgitates into the baby's oesophagus, causing irritation and pain – it's a bit like heart-burn. This is more likely to happen when your baby is lying down; in such cases they will be happier sitting up. Your baby may be 'sicky', with milk coming back up through the mouth or nose – or both. However, sometimes this isn't apparent, as the milk only regurgitates part of the way up the oesophagus.

What you can do

After each feed, put your baby in a sling and carry them around with you. The closeness, motion, and upright position will soothe and relax them, and promote good digestion.

CHECKLIST OF WHAT WE'VE COVERED

In this chapter we've looked at:

♥ What baby colic is, and how your baby could be feeling

♥ Ways to identify the stages of colic and their possible symptoms and causes

♥ How some foods could be affecting your milk, food intolerances and sensitivities, and some common food culprits.

WHAT IS BABY COLIC?

BABY COLIC HELP

CHAPTER TWO
WHAT YOU CAN DO FOR YOUR BABY

PART ONE

In this chapter we're going to look at some ways to soothe and calm your troubled baby.

When faced with a distressed and crying baby, it can be hard to know where to start. I recommend that you begin with a quick Baby's Needs Check or BNC.

BABY'S NEEDS CHECK

Is your baby...

- Tired
- Hungry
- Thirsty
- Too hot or cold
- In pain or uncomfortable
- Not latching onto the breast or bottle properly
- Over-stimulated or under-stimulated. Late afternoon / evening is a time when babies are prone to either be over-stimulated, needing time out, or under-stimulated, needing quality time with you
- Just needing a cuddle?

Sometimes we can run through all these checks and still find there is nothing we can do to 'fix' things. In such cases, I suggest doing some Facilitated Crying (see the next chapter, WHAT YOU CAN DO FOR YOUR BABY PART TWO) – in other words letting them cry, and say what they have to say, while also keeping them safe, comfortable and reassured.

WHAT YOU CAN DO FOR YOUR BABY

> **CAUTION**
>
> If your baby is running a high temperature (above 39 degrees centigrade or higher), extremely distressed, projectile vomiting, or has unexplained rashes or blemishes, you need to get medical advice as soon as possible.

WATCH THE WIND

PREVENTING A WINDY BABY

Swallowing excess air could be contributing to how uncomfortable your baby is feeling. Whether you are breast feeding or bottle feeding, there are ways to prevent this.

BREAST FEEDING TIPS

Make sure your baby is latched on properly. Position your baby square on to the breast with their face facing the breast. (To appreciate the importance of this, just try to drink from a glass of water with your neck twisted!) Don't worry, your baby can breathe! Try to get your baby's lips to make a good seal far back on the areola (the darker area) around the nipple.

- ♡ Be aware that if your wearing strong perfume or deodorant it may be too over-powering for your baby; and, as the ampit is close to the breast, you find they appear unhappy when put to the breast.

Let baby finish one breast before you offer the other one. When you feel that you're running out of a good flow of milk on one side then move them to the other breast.

> ## OVERACTIVE MILK LET-DOWN
>
> An overactive let-down can cause colic. Sometimes breast milk can literally spray into baby's mouth too quickly. Try lying down while breastfeeding so excess milk can run down the side of the baby's mouth. Expressing some milk before breastfeeding can also be helpful; however, try to avoid doing this if possible, as the best quality milk is at the beginning of the feed.

BOTTLE-FEEDING TIPS

Anti-colic teats and bottles simulate the natural flex, feel, and movement of the breast as the baby feeds. They can help to reduce the amount of air being swallowed.

Adjust the bottle position, tilting the bottle at an angle of between 30 – 40 degrees, so the air rises to the bottom of the bottle. Position the bottle with your baby's lips on the wide base of the nipple teat, not just the tip.

BURPING

If you think your baby is showing this Stage 1 symptom (see Chapter One: WHAT IS BABY COLIC?), then the problems could be due to trapped wind in the stomach. In this case, burping techniques can be extremely helpful.

WHAT YOU CAN DO FOR YOUR BABY

- Directly after feeding, sit your baby on your knee. Avoid sitting them in a scrunched-up position, as this may worsen the problem by keeping the wind trapped.
- Gently pat the middle of the back, level with the tummy, followed by a gentle circular massage with the palm of your hand to the same area of the back.
- Repeat the patting and massaging, going slowly up and down the back.

You can also try patting and massaging the baby's back while they're leaning over your shoulder or lying face down across your legs. Different positions work better for different babies. Sometimes you'll need to try all three: sitting baby on your knee, laying them over your shoulder, and laying them face down across your legs.

CRYING... CRYING... CRYING!!!

Even non-colicky babies can spend two to three hours crying a day. Why do we feel so disturbed when we hear a baby crying, even if the baby is not ours? Research shows that hearing the sound of a baby crying can trigger unique emotional responses in our brains. Almost instantly – about as long as it takes to blink – primitive parts of the brain react. These are the parts of the brain that are connected to our fight or flight responses, and they cause us to feel alert and ready for action. If we can't respond with effective action – we're unable to help the crying baby – we feel disturbed or irritated. Is any of this sounding familiar?

It's natural, then, to want calm a crying baby, espcially when it's our own child and we can feel that we're letting them down if we don't succeed in stopping their crying. This is when it's good to remember that, if all else fails, there is still another approach that we can take: Facilitated Crying. (There's more about this in Chapter Three: WHAT YOU CAN DO FOR YOUR BABY PART TWO.)

It's also good to bear in mind that a baby's cries aren't just meaningless noises; they differ depending on the baby's needs at the time. They are a language! A system developed by an Australian woman, Priscilla Dunstan, called the Dunstan Baby Language System, has helped many parents learn to listen to what their baby is saying. You may find her DVDs helpful (details in the Further Resources section at the end of this book).

THE POWER OF TOUCH

Loving touch is a universal way of expressing love. With a simple, kind touch of the hand we can deeply connect with another being, communicate our feelings, and give and receive love. Touch helps us to feel nurtured and nourished in our lives, and a cuddle can comfort, heal, and lift our spirits. Touch is a baby's most powerful sense: the skin is the first organ to develop, and even in the womb there is a sense of touch.

For a crying baby, there's no greater comfort than to be lovingly touched and held. Touch is like food for babies – they need it! So we all have this powerful therapeutic tool at our fingertips. Baby massage is an ancient tradition throughout the world, including Indian, Tibetan, Malaysian, Chinese and African cultures, for improving infant health and wellbeing. And, in the animal kingdom, this expression of love can surely not be missed: almost all species touch in some way to communicate, bond, form groups and colonies, and to help to promote natural growth and wellbeing.

We often say, 'Let's rub it better', to reassure a child who has been hurt. It's a natural reaction to stroke the area of skin that has been affected. By caring and giving love through touch, you can powerfully help to heal by encouraging the natural repair process: blood and oxygen are brought to the damaged area, while swelling and inflammation are reduced by the body's production of its own corticosteroids as well as endorphins, which are natural painkillers.

BABY MASSAGE

Soothing massage can be so helpful to bring relief and relaxation that it has its own chapter! (See Chapter Four: IN YOUR LOVING HANDS.)

SOOTHING SUGGESTIONS

Here are some ideas for you to try when your baby is crying. You can find detailed instructions for how to do each technique following the list of suggestions.

- ♥ WARM HANDS TECHNIQUE
- ♥ COLON CIRCLES
- ♥ WINDING DOWN TIME
- ♥ HOLD YOUR BABY CLOSE
- ♥ BABY MASSAGE (see Chapter Four: IN YOUR LOVING HANDS).

1. WARM HANDS TECHNIQUE

This simple technique can be very useful when your baby is feeling slightly fretful and in need of some comfort and calming.

HERE'S HOW TO DO IT

- ♥ Take a relaxing breath, then rub your hands together to generate some heat into them.
- ♥ Next, place your hands onto your baby's abdomen (see diagram) and rest them there for a while.
- ♥ Send calm, loving thoughts through your hands and enjoy the loving connection between you both. You may be surprised how comforted and relaxed your baby can become by your doing something so simple.

BABY COLIC HELP

WARM HANDS TECHNIQUE

2. COLON CIRCLES (Releasing Technique)

This gentle but firm massage (give yourself a little massage to help you gauge what it feels like, remembering that you need to be very gentle with a young baby!) to the baby's abdomen can be very soothing and relaxing for tight muscles, which could be restricting natural wind from moving more freely through the colon. If you suspect your baby is at stage 2 (see the previous chapter) this Releasing Technique can help. The problems could be below the stomach, more in the small and large intestine / colon area, with a number of reasons for the discomfort, including trapped wind, constipation, tight abdominal muscles, general tension and immature myelination of the nerves.

HERE'S HOW TO DO IT

- Start your massage under your baby's rib cage, down near the hip on their right side; this is where the colon begins (see diagram).
- Using your flat hand or your fingers, massage with one hand clockwise in one large circular flowing movement from one side of your baby's abdomen to the other (see diagram).
- Now use the other hand do the same, before resuming massaging with the first hand again. Using both hands

WHAT YOU CAN DO FOR YOUR BABY

like this will create a steady circular movement that will help to soothe and relieve congestion and discomfort within the colon and surrounding muscles. (See the information on the vagus nerve in Chapter One: WHAT IS BABY COLIC?)

COLON CIRCLES

WINDING DOWN TIME

Establishing a routine that includes a winding down time in the evening can help your baby to learn that it's time to unwind and relax before being put to bed.

HERE'S HOW TO DO IT

- ♥ Try giving your baby a warm bath, followed by a lovely gentle massage (see Chapter Four: IN YOUR LOVING HANDS) or perhaps some gentle baby yoga stretches (see Chapter Five: BABY YOGA).
- ♥ Make sure their bedroom is conducive to relaxation. Shut the curtains, dim the lights and remove any brightly coloured toys from the cot (bright colours are stimulating).
- ♥ Try some soothing relaxation music at bedtime; this can help some babies to unwind and fall asleep. Plus, leaving

BABY COLIC HELP

them to go to sleep with the gentle sound of music can help them to learn to relax without you at other times of day.

HOLD YOUR BABY CLOSE

Try wrapping your baby in a blanket or shawl, or use a sling to carry them close to you as you go about your day. Try sitting or lying together, for a while. Skin to skin contact has been found to help babies cry less and sleep better. Have a bath together, and sit or lie with your baby directly on your skin; they will find comfort in your smell and the sound of your heart beat.

Newborn babies have limited control over their neuro-muscular activity and can experience the 'Moro reflex' when they are startled – their arms and legs move quickly and randomly around. Swaddling your baby can help to reduce this (see diagram).

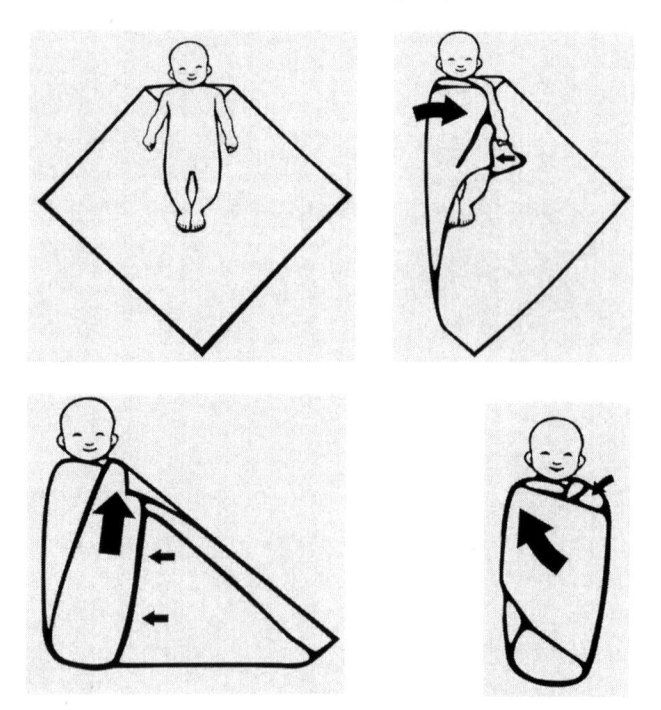

DO I SWADDLE?

References to swaddling go back to biblical times and the practice is still common in many cultures. For nine months your baby has been beautifully cocooned, nourished and safe in the womb. In the latter stage of pregnancy, as space within the womb becomes increasingly limited, your baby has become accustomed to gaining comfort from containment. When a gentle calming voice doesn't suffice to comfort your baby, hugging or swaddling could help. Your baby gets to feel warm and cossetted, reminding them of the womb, and this may help them to settle and relax..

As a point of safety, it's important to use a swaddling material that can breathe so that your baby doesn't overheat. Something like muslin is ideal.

There are varying professional view points on the safety of swaddling and I suggest you talk to your midwife or health visitor and look at the NHS, Baby Centre, and National Childbirth Trust websites before you make your decision.

FURTHER SOOTHING SUGGESTIONS

MOVEMENT
Some babies find comfort in movement. You might experiment with:

- Using a sling
- Taking them out in the pram
- Giving them a ride in the car
- Practising some baby yoga movement combined with song). (See Chapter Five: BABY YOGA.)

SOUND / MUSIC

Some babies settle when exposed to repetitive sound. The sound of the car, the vacuum cleaner or even the rhythm of the washing machine can gently distract them and help them to relax. It's amazing how powerful music can be to distract, relax and uplift your baby. Try putting on some relaxing music or some baby songs.

CHECKLIST OF WHAT WE'VE COVERED IN PART ONE

In this chapter we've looked at:

- ♥ First, do the Baby Needs Check (BNC) as some reasons for the crying can be easily put right

- ♥ Watch the Wind – tips for breast feeding and bottle feeding

- ♥ Try some burping techniques to make sure that wind is not causing discomfort

- ♥ Dealing with constant crying

- ♥ The Power of Touch – why it's so important

- ♥ Baby Massage (details in Chapter Four: IN YOUR LOVING HANDS).

- ♥ Soothing Suggestions – the Warm Hands Technique helps to comfort and settle and Colon Circles (Releasing Technique) help alleviate and release tension and wind.

- ♥ Wind Down Time – ideas and suggestions

- ♥ Think about trying swaddling to give your baby extra comfort

- ♥ Further Soothing Suggestions – Movement and Sound / Music

BABY COLIC HELP

CHAPTER THREE
WHAT YOU CAN DO FOR YOUR BABY

PART TWO

In this chapter we're going to continue with suggestions for ways to soothe and calm your troubled baby. We'll look at birth stress, facilitated crying, how to identify tongue-tie, how to understand your baby's ways of communication and some pros and cons of using a dummy.

BIRTH STRESS

Some stress is good – at the beginning of labour it actually helps to stimulate the creation of massive numbers of neurons in the brain, so your baby's brain is primed for new learning once it is born.

If, however, there's a difficult birth or post-birth trauma, stress hormones could continue to stay high after the birth, which could affect your baby adversely. It may lead to your baby's withdrawing into long periods of sleep, being unsettled and irritable, or not being very interactive, for example not smiling, not gazing at you, or being unresponsive.

SOME SIGNS OF POSSIBLE BIRTH STRESS

- Excessive crying
- Constant crying (check this with your GP)
- Poor sleep
- Difficulties when feeding, or with latching on
- Constant demands to suckle
- Unsettled
- Colicky
- Trapped wind
- Acid reflux
- Asthma or breathing problems
- Crying when lying on their back (check this with your GP)
- Floppy or rigid baby (check this with your GP)
- Unresponsive baby (check this with your GP).

WAYS TO REDUCE STRESS LEVELS

- **MAKING EYE CONTACT**
  Sit or lie close, and spend some time gazing into your baby's beautiful eyes.

- **HAVING MORE SKIN CONTACT**
  Cuddling, and a soothing stroke or massage – loving touch is nurturing and nourishing.

- **FEELING YOUR BREATH, HEARING YOUR HEARTBEAT**
  Sit or lie together; have your baby close to you; gently cuddle and rock them. Rhythmic swaying and motion can have a profoundly calming effect on our nerves and emotions.

- **SMELLING YOU**
  Avoid using perfume or strong deodorants; let your baby smell the real you. Your familiar smell can help to calm them. Familiar smells can powerfully evoke warm, comforting feelings.

- **HEARING THE SOUND OF YOUR VOICE**
  Chat to your baby in a kind and gentle way; you can talk about anything – it doesn't need to make logical sense! Ask them questions and look for their responses through sound or body language. They will love it!

FACILITATED CRYING

Women and men are naturally wired to respond to the sound of a baby crying – any baby, not just their own baby! We react instinctively. We want to help and to calm them, and, if we're unable to do this, we may feel irritated, upset and even feel we have failed in some way.

However, if you've done your Baby's Needs Check and ruled out any medical concerns, and still your baby is crying, let's consider another way of looking at your baby's need to cry.

It could be that they just need to share how they feel, without being told to 'shhhh'! How would you feel if you went to someone you trusted to share your feelings and they just told you to stop crying, calm down, and be quiet – and then stuck something in your mouth to pacify you! Holding on to unresolved feelings will eventually sap anyone's energy and dampen their spirits; such feelings need to be safely released, not suppressed.

Your baby may need to tell you their story, perhaps about their birth experience, or how uncomfortable they are feeling, or they may just have something that they need to 'cry out' of their system. Facilitated crying is about giving your baby the space and time to do just that. They need to feel heard, as we all do from time to time, so you give them your patience and kind attention and let them say whatever it is they have to say. It's likely that when they have expressed themselves they will naturally quieten and feel better.

Allowing your little one to experience these healthy emotional releases will help them to be a happier baby. It may also help them to grow up with more emotional maturity, so that when they experience life's natural ups and downs they will be better equipped to express and manage difficult emotions and feelings.

HOW TO DO IT

- Sit or lie in a comfortable position with your baby, so you can get good eye-to-eye contact, and take a couple of good deep breaths.
- Now let them cry; they are telling you their story.
- Encourage them to do this by speaking gently, telling them that you are here and listening. This will reassure them that it's safe to release how they feel and, most importantly, that they are being heard.
- You may find that, after a little while, the crying will lose its strength or even stop. Even if they continue to cry and you decide to stop the facilitated crying session, they will still have felt heard and cared for. We all need to feel

heard and this will help to strengthen their sense of self worth and wellbeing.
- Finish this time with a lovely cuddle together.

TONGUE-TIE

Tongue-tie (ankyloglossia) is when the piece of skin joining the tongue to the base of the mouth is short or tight. It restricts tongue movement and makes it hard for your baby to latch on properly when feeding. Reports have shown that tongue-tie can affect between 4 – 5 % newborm (Messener et al., 2000; Riche et al., 2005) and the NHS suggests, it can affect up to as much as 10% of babies. Tongue-tied babies tend to slide off the breast and chomp on the nipple with their gums, often causing soreness and pain to the breast. Poor feeding can lead to hungry and irritable babies. Tongue-tie is a very simple procedure to correct; if you think your baby may have it, speak to your doctor or health visitor or find a breast-feeding group where you can get some information.

WHAT'S YOUR BABY SAYING?

Research shows that a high percentage of our communication occurs through non-verbal body language – and this applies to babies as well.

Your baby speaks to you in two main ways, through sound and body language. As you learn to read your baby's signs, you'll be better able to deal with situations and ensure they are comfortable, happy and peaceful.

THE MORO REFLEX

This is a natural response that can occur if the baby is startled – the legs and arms suddenly stretch out and move, giving the impression your baby is alarmed. This could be due to sensitivity to sudden noise; some babies are more sensitive than others.

ROOTING

Whether hungry or not, when babies feel something rubbing at the corner of their mouths, they open wide and 'root' in that direction, turning their heads and forming their mouths into funny lopsided O's, in the hope that a teat will be presented. And often it is!

ARCHING THE BACK

Babies often arch their back while keeping their eyes wide open due to physical pain and discomfort. You may notice your baby does this when he or she is experiencing colic or bouts of gas. The fingers and toes may be flexed, and your baby may let out a loud cry.

KICKING THE LEGS

Some babies kick their legs because they are happy or they want to be picked up in order to see you face to face. If your baby is kicking his or her legs, this is a great time to play.

TIREDNESS

Babies can show their tiredness in many ways, for example:

- Rubbing the eyes
- Drooping the eyelids and blinking slowly
- Making stiff and jerky movements
- Whining and being irritable, fretful and cranky.

OVER-STIMULATED OR JUST HAD ENOUGH PLAY

There are times when your baby is having fun and enjoying being played with, but then suddenly starts to fuss, bringing their hands up to block their faces or merely looking away. This could be a sign they've been stimulated enough and are unable to cope with any more. If you respect their cues, stop playing, and calm everything down, you'll have a happier, more peaceful baby who will find it easier to 'clock off' and sleep at those very important times.

DO I USE A DUMMY?

The use of dummies, also called pacifiers, is something many parents feel very strongly about – either for or against. You may have seen dummies being used more as silencers than comforters, leaving quite a negative impression on you and putting you firmly in the 'against' camp. But now that you're faced with a crying, uncomfortable, inconsolable baby, you might be reconsidering.

Dummies should never be forced on the baby and it's considered best not to give them to a baby under a month old.

PROS AND CONS TO HELP YOU DECIDE

THE *PROS* FOR USING A DUMMY

- **TO SOOTHE**
  Most babies have a strong sucking reflex. They can be seen sucking their thumbs or fingers in the womb. Babies often suck to calm or soothe themselves, especially when troubled by colic.

- **FOR DISTRACTION**
  A dummy might come in handy to distract the baby during procedures such as vaccinations and blood tests.

- **IT MAY HELP SOME BABIES SLEEP**
  If your baby has trouble settling down, a dummy might do the trick.

- **IT MAY REDUCE THE RISK OF SUDDEN INFANT DEATH SYNDROME (SIDS)**
  Research has found an association between dummy use during sleep and a reduced risk of SIDS.

- **DUMMIES ARE DISPOSABLE**
  When it's time to stop using dummies, you can throw them away. If your child prefers sucking on their thumb or fingers, it might be more difficult to break the habit.

THE CONS AGAINST USING A DUMMY

- **DEPENDENCY**
  Your baby might become dependent on the dummy. If your baby uses a dummy to sleep, you might face frequent middle-of-the-night crying spells when the dummy falls out of their mouth.

- **RISK OF A MIDDLE EAR INFECTION**
  Using a dummy might increase the risk of middle ear infection. However this risk is balanced by the fact that rates of middle ear infection are generally lowest from birth to age six months — which is when the risk of SIDS is the highest and also when your baby might be most interested in a dummy.

- **DENTAL PROBLEMS**
  Normal dummy use during the first few years of life doesn't cause long-term dental problems. However, prolonged dummy use might cause a child's top front teeth to slant outward. To avoid this, aim to discard the dummy before your child is one year old. To prevent decay never put sugary stuff on a dummy.

- ♡ **SPEAKING PROBLEMS**
  Research suggests that children sucking their fingers, a bottle or a dummy past the age of three may develop problems with speaking.

- ♡ **HINDERING SOCIAL SKILLS**
  Prolonged use of a dummy during waking hours could prevent the child from joining in the chatter of everyday conversation, thereby reducing the opportunities to start learning important social skills.

NATURAL REMEDIES FOR COLIC

You may like to know about some other alternative ways to help calm and soothe your baby. Natural health professionals often recommend the following remedies. You'll need to check with a qualified therapist about how to use them.

CHAMOMILLA GRANULES 30/60c

This is a homoeopathic remedy which is said to relax tight muscles (anti-spasmodic) and calm the nerves. It can be given to your baby directly or put on to the nipple before a feed.

BACH FLOWER ESSENCES

These remedies are made from extracts from flowers. They are believed to have a positive effect on emotional imbalances.

Bach Flower mix 90, used daily, could help your baby to feel less sensitive and upset and become calmer and more peaceful.

Bach Night Rescue Remedy is an alcohol-free combination of relaxing and calming Bach Flower essences. It could improve your baby's sleep by calming the emotions and reducing anxiety.

AVENA SATIVA COMP. DROPS

Avena Sativa (also known as oats and oat straw) is a wonderful calming herb.

ESSENTIAL OILS

Either lavender or chamomile essential oil can help to relax your baby's muscles and nervous system, calm the mind and promote peaceful sleep. Try putting a drop onto a tissue or blanket and place it in the cot at night, or put a few drops in your baby's bath. One or two drops could be used in a essential oil diffuser to help create a calm and relaxed environment in your house or in the baby's room. It's best to use only 100% pure essential oils.

CHECKLIST OF WHAT WE'VE COVERED IN PART TWO

In this chapter we've looked at:

- ♡ Birth stress and symptoms, and suggestions on different ways to reduce stress levels

- ♡ Facilitated crying

- ♡ Tongue-tie

- ♡ Understanding your baby's communication

- ♡ Dummies and the pros and cons

- ♡ Natural remedies.

BABY COLIC HELP

CHAPTER FOUR
IN YOUR LOVING HANDS

In this chapter we're going to look at the benefits of baby massage, and there are instructions for a baby colic massage routine for you to try.

THE ART OF BABY MASSAGE

Baby massage is an ancient art, deeply rooted in many cultures, that helps you to connect with this new little person. Through giving positive touch, you also receive: it's a wonderful opportunity to nurture and nourish your baby, getting to know him or her better on all levels, while feeling good yourself.

There's no hard and fast rule about when you can start to massage your baby. Initially, it may be more beneficial for your baby to experience a gentle, nurturing touch such as the 'warm hands' technique (see Chapter Two: WHAT YOU CAN DO FOR YOUR BABY PART ONE), rather than trying too many massage techniques, which might be a bit overwhelming. However, you are the best judge of this. Some small, gentle massage movements on the feet and hands could be very relaxing and soothing and just what they need right now. Don't be afraid to discover what comes naturally to you, as you will be very 'tuned in' to your baby and are likely to know intuitively what is best for them.

Why not invite other members of the family to try some baby massage? It's wonderful coming from mums, dads, siblings (supervised), carers and other family members, too!

BENEFITS OF BABY MASSAGE

Baby massage can help to:

- ♥ Empower you by helping you to understand your baby better
- ♥ Improve the general functioning of your baby's immune system
- ♥ Regulate and strengthen the digestive system (which may reduce the discomfort of colic, wind and constipation)
- ♥ Promote relaxation and improve quality of sleep

- ♥ Reduce pain through increasing endorphins, a natural painkiller
- ♥ Reduce levels of cortisol (stress hormone)
- ♥ Alleviate wind and constipation
- ♥ Strengthen the bond between you and your baby
- ♥ Balance the nervous system
- ♥ Boost the respiratory system
- ♥ Release the relaxing 'feel good' hormone oxytocin
- ♥ Help your baby to grow and flourish.

HOW TO PRACTISE BABY MASSAGE

SIMPLE KIT

You will need:

- ♥ A towel
- ♥ A blanket or changing mat
- ♥ Massage oil.

> ### MASSAGE OILS
>
> Fractionated Coconut oil, Almond oil, Grapeseed oil and Sunflower oil are all good to use with babies. Fractionated Coconut oil is slightly easier to use and has a longer shelf life.
>
> If your baby has broken skin or very sensitive skin, it's best to do a skin test first: put a little oil on the inside of their wrist and then wait 24 hours to see if there is any reaction.
>
> Keep your oil free of fragrance, as your baby

> only needs to smell you! Also, some essential oils are not safe to use on babies.
>
> The following preparations can help to make massage-time more enjoyable for you and your baby.

PREPARING THE ROOM

- ♡ Turn off the TV and radio – your baby just needs to see and hear your voice, and not be over-stimulated or distracted.
- ♡ Make sure the room is warm and your baby is not lying in a draught.
- ♡ Avoid bright lights over-head – if there is a bright light above your head it may shine uncomfortably in your baby's eyes and make it difficult for the two of you to make good eye contact.
- ♡ Find a safe and firm base, for example a carpeted floor or a firm bed; make sure it's in a position that will be comfortable for you too.
- ♡ If possible, pick a time when the room is quiet, so that you can have special one-to-one time.

PREPARING YOURSELF

- ♡ Remove any jewellery, especially anything sharp.
- ♡ Have a nice relaxing stretch and take a couple of deep breaths. This helps you to release any stress or tension as your baby could easily pick up on your mood.
- ♡ Make sure you're comfortable in a massaging position which is nice and close to your baby: be careful about your posture, especially bending over – you need to

look after your back.
- I suggest that, before you begin, you take a couple of deep, slow, relaxing breaths, then loosen your shoulders by doing a few shoulder shrugs.

PREPARING YOUR BABY

- **CHOOSE A GOOD TIME**
  Choose a period when your baby is not too tired or hungry. Don't wake them up to give them a massage! A good time may be after a sleep, when they're ready for some activity or before or after a bath. Try some different times; see what works best for you both. If your baby is crying or seems to be colicky, you can try a little massage and see how they respond – if the crying persists, try massaging a different area, and if nothing works, stop the massage and try a cuddle instead!

- **ASK PERMISSION**
  This means you get some eye contact and ask your baby whether they are happy to try a massage. They will make it known if they are not! Perhaps surprisingly, they will have a subtle understanding of what you are asking. Your baby will respond to your question either vocally or with body language. Check the *What's Your Baby Saying?* section in Chapter Three: WHAT YOU CAN DO FOR YOUR BABY PART TWO, if you need guidance in understanding their communication; if it's still difficult to be sure, just try a little massage and see how they respond.

- **NEVER FORCE**
  Don't impose a massage on your baby. If they're not enjoying it, stop! You can always try again another time.

♡ **NAPPY- FREE**
   It's better for the baby to be nappy free for massage, but not essential.

THE BABY COLIC MASSAGE ROUTINE

Apply a small amount of oil to the palms of your hands and lightly rub them together to warm both your hands and the oil.

THE FOLLOWING SEQUENCE OF MASSAGE TECHNIQUES IS SUGGESTED:

1. **WARM HANDS TECHNIQUE**

Take a relaxing breath, then rub your hands together to generate some heat into them. Next, place your hands onto your baby's abdomen (see diagram) and rest them there for a while.

Send calm, loving thoughts through your hands and enjoy the loving connection between you both. You may be surprised how comforted and relaxed your baby can become by your doing something so simple.

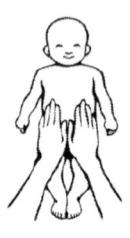

WARM HANDS TECHNIQUE

2. **TUMMY STROKES**

Starting just below the bottom of your baby's ribcage, using alternate hands, massage with your palms over the abdomen with a downward movement (see diagram). If your baby is nappy free you can easily massage down on to your baby's thighs. This will further help relax and stretch the Psoas muscles. Repeat 4 times.

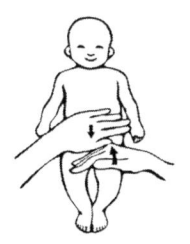

TUMMY STROKES

3. COLON CIRCLES (Releasing Technique)

Starting on the tummy down near the hip on their right side, using your flat hand or your fingers, massage with one hand clockwise in one large circular flowing movement from one side of your baby's abdomen to the other (see diagram). Do the same with the other hand, then go back to the first hand again, so you're using both hands in a steady circular movement.

COLON CIRCLES

BABY COLIC HELP

> ## CAUTION!
>
> If your baby has any spinal, hip or leg problems which are being treated or are under professional supervision, do check with your doctor or health visitor first before doing any of the baby massage or yoga exercises.

4. KNEE BENDS AND CIRCLES

Gently cupping the knees in your hands, take them up towards the tummy (see diagram), and do some small circles in a clockwise direction (see diagram). Then gently release the legs back down straight again and give them a gentle little stretch. Repeat 2 – 4 times.

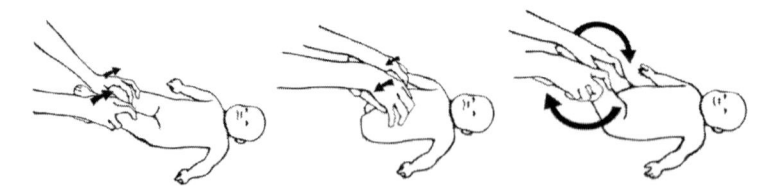

KNEE BENDS AND CIRCLES

5. COLON STRETCHES

Starting at the lower right hand corner of your baby's abdomen, at the bottom of the colon, massage gently and firmly up the right side (from the baby's point of view) of the abdomen along the upward path of the colon (see diagram). Continue massaging in a straight line across the top of the abdomen from the baby's right to left, along the top of the colon (see diagram) and then down (see diagram). Repeat this 2 – 4 times.

This is a wonderful massage for helping the movement of (faecal material) waste and wind through the colon, while also helping to relax the muscles.

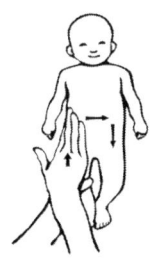

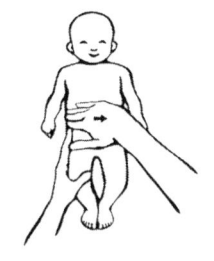

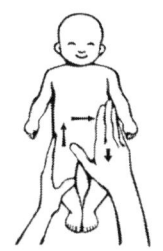

COLON STRETCHES

REPEAT **KNEE BENDS AND CIRCLES**
REPEAT **TUMMY STROKES**
Repeat the tummy strokes.

6. **INTEGRAL STROKE**

Place your hands on your baby's tummy (see diagram) and stroke down to the feet (see diagram). This massage stroke helps to stretch out the muscles and is soothing and comforting. It's a lovely massage to finish with. Repeat 2 – 3 times.

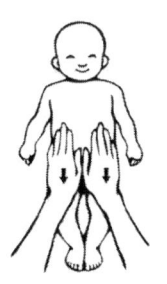

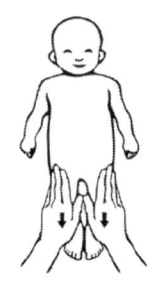

INTEGRAL STROKE

Your colic routine can stop here, with the Integral Stroke, but if you want to do more, or if your baby is uncomfortable with an abdominal massage, you can carry on with a back massage.

THE BACK MASSAGE ROUTINE

It's possible that your baby may not feel comfortable enough to let you massage their abdomen but would be happy to lie on their front, across your legs, or on your chest or on your shoulder, for a back massage. When your baby is experiencing colicky symptoms the lower back muscles can be very tight and uncomfortable, so massaging the back, especially the lower back, could be very soothing and relaxing.

Back massage can also be beneficial to the nerves emerging from the spinal cord, including those nerves which send essential messages to the digestive system including the stomach and small and large intestines.

7. CRISS-CROSS STROKE

Lay your baby across your legs and massage back and forth across the back, working gently over the spine (see diagram).

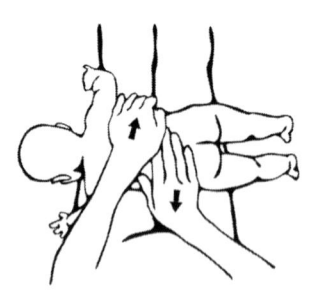

CRISS-CROSS STROKE

8. FINGER CIRCLES

Massage with your fingers working in circles on either side of the spine, then over the buttocks (see diagram). This technique could also be used around the neck and shoulders for releasing tension in those areas.

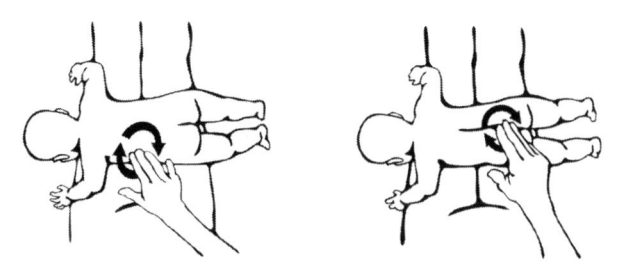

FINGER CIRCLES

9. EFFLEURAGE (stroking technique)

Using your whole hand, stroke down your baby's back several times. When stroking with one hand, rest the other hand very gently on your baby's head, neck or back, to ensure your baby stays safely on your legs (see diagram).

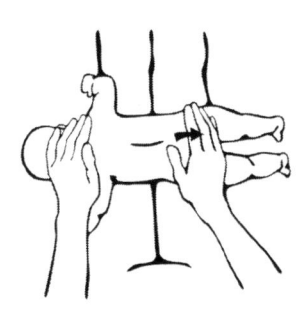

EFFLEURAGE

BABY COLIC HELP

10. INTEGRAL STROKE

As you did before, when you were massaging your baby's front, here you continue stroking down the legs, but this time on the back of the body and legs (see diagram).

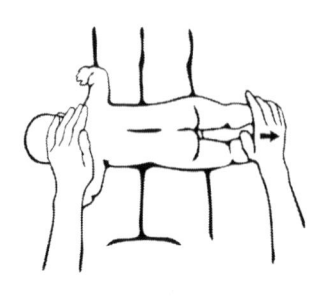

INTEGRAL STROKE

THE COLIC MASSAGE ROUTINE SUMMARISED

1. Warm Hands Technique
2. Tummy Strokes 4 times
3. Colon Circles
4. Knee Bends and Circles 2 – 4 times
   Repeat Colon Circles
   Repeat Knee Bends
5. Colon Stretches 2 – 4 times
   Repeat Knee Bends and Circles
   Repeat Tummy Strokes
6. Integral Strokes 2 – 4 times

OPTIONAL

BACK MASSAGE

7. Criss-Cross Stroke 6 times
8. Finger Circles 4 times

9. Effleurage 2 – 4 times
10. Integral Stroke 2 – 4 times
    Finish with a cuddle!

For getting the maximum benefit from the colic massage it's ideal to repeat numbers 1 – 6 once or twice up to four times a day if your baby is happy and not too tired or hungry. But don't worry if you don't manage to get through the whole routine or do it more than once – anything you do is great!

You might like to look into joining a baby group so that you can meet and talk to other parents and carers, learn more massage techniques and have some fun.

COMMENTS FROM MASSAGING MUMS

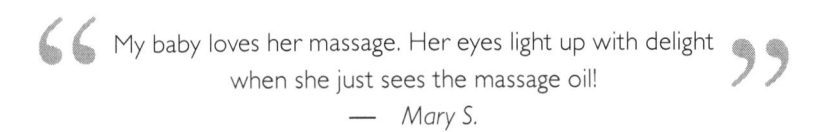

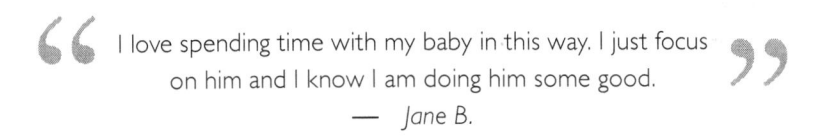

> My baby loves her massage. Her eyes light up with delight when she just sees the massage oil!
> — Mary S.

> I love spending time with my baby in this way. I just focus on him and I know I am doing him some good.
> — Jane B.

> I feel as if I have something to try, so I don't feel so helpless and stressed all the time. Massaging in the evening has really helped my baby to sleep longer and he is generally more restful.
> — Sam F.

> I am proud of myself for being proactive and doing something to try to help.
> — Gemma S.

> I feel more confident handling and massaging my baby and she seems to respond better towards me afterwards.
> — Tracey W.

COMMENTS FROM DADS TOO

> Now our baby is happier I don't worry so much about my wife having to deal with everything all day alone – and I look forward to coming home now.
> — Steve S.

> I was so disappointed and angry that being a parent was so stressful but, now she is more relaxed, we have fun and I adore being with our baby.
> — Graham B.

CHECKLIST OF WHAT WE'VE COVERED

In this chapter we've looked at:

♡ The art of baby massage – some background on massage and its benefits

♡ Preparation – guidelines for you to follow before a massage

♡ A baby colic massage routine – a sequence of massage techniques for you to follow.

BABY COLIC HELP

CHAPTER FIVE
BABY YOGA

In this chapter we're going to look at some gentle physical exercises you can do with your baby.

WHAT IS BABY YOGA?

Baby yoga consists of gentle stretching exercises. The exercises are often combined with a simple song or two. This is a fun time to spend with your baby; babies love song – and they don't mind how you sound! And if you can get other family members involved too, so much the better!

BENEFITS OF BABY YOGA

- It strengthens bonding between you and your baby.
- It helps to build your confidence in handling and understanding your baby.
- It feels good for you both; you have quality fun time together.
- It stimulates the whole brain development.
- It improves the general functioning of the immune system.
- It improves the quality of your baby's sleep.
- It helps to release the relaxing hormone oxytocin in your baby.

Why not think about joining a class? This could be a fun way to learn and practise exercises with others.

Baby yoga can help with some common difficulties, including:

- Trapped wind
- Teething discomfort
- Constipation and digestive problems
- Slow weight gain
- Feeding difficulties
- Poor sleeping patterns
- Fretfulness and general tension.

STAGE 3 COLIC

I have found that Stage 3 colic can be related to ongoing spinal and muscular tension due to the position of the baby during the later stages of pregnancy, from the birthing experience, or just from general tightness being held in the spine and abdomen. Both massage and baby yoga exercises are extremely helpful to relax your baby's spine and release tension spots in the colon and surrounding areas. Ideally, repeat the massages and exercises at least three to four times a day.

BABY YOGA EXERCISES

As well as being fun, these exercises could be helpful for alleviating discomfort during a bout of colic. However, if you baby appears to be unhappy with them, stop and try another time.

If your baby is a newborn just do little movements.

I'm suggesting some songs to accompany these exercises but they can, of course, be replaced with any songs that you prefer. Singing anything will really help to focus and lift the mood for you both. Don't worry about your singing voice – your baby will just love to hear you, whatever comes out!

BABY COLIC HELP

1. WHEELS ON THE BUS – Knee Circles

Lay your baby on their back on a comfortable, safe surface. Cupping the knees, gently bring them up towards the tummy, then circle the legs in a clockwise direction (see diagram). This will give the abdomen a little massage and stretch the lower spine, giving some relief and helping to move trapped wind. Be warned – you could get a few gassy explosions at this point!

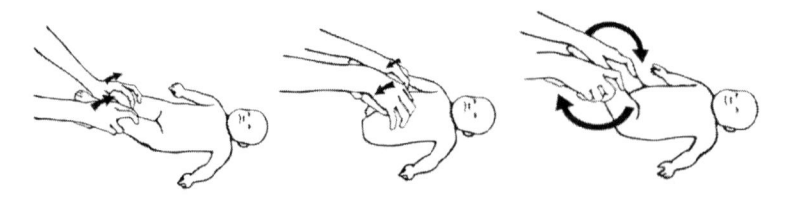

WHEELS ON THE BUS / KNEE CIRCLES

2. TICK TOCK – Brain Gym

This is an across-the-body stretch, a good whole brain exercise.

Holding your baby's diagonally-opposite hand and leg (see diagram), gently bring their hand across the body towards the opposite hip, while at the same time taking their foot towards the opposite shoulder so you can touch the hand to the foot (see diagram). Then stretch the arm and leg outwards before doing the same movement on the other side. Repeat both sides 2 or 3 times. This exercise helps to stretch the abdominal muscles and is also good for the Psoas muscles. It also gives your baby 'whole brain' stimulation which is good for their natural development.

BABY YOGA

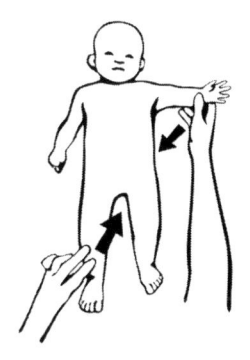

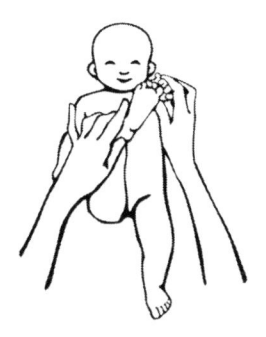

TICK TOCK

3. I LIKE TO RIDE MY BICYCLE – Pedaling

This exercise involves bending and straightening alternate legs. Cup one knee (see diagram) and bring the leg up towards the body; then straighten it again as you bring up the other leg (see diagram). Pedaling is good for stretching the Psoas muscles, and the baby's little thighs touching the abdomen can give the colon a massage. Bending the knees up like this will give your baby some relief from discomfort.

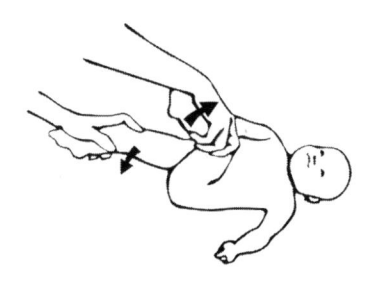

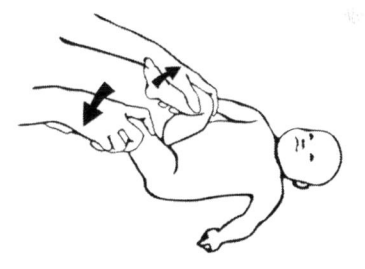

PEDALING

HERE ARE COMMENTS FROM PARENTS

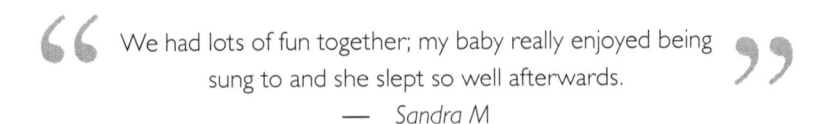

> We had lots of fun together; my baby really enjoyed being sung to and she slept so well afterwards.
> — Sandra M

> I was unsure at first how I would feel about doing baby yoga. I didn't sing much, but I really enjoyed the exercises and my little chap couldn't stop smiling!
> — Nigel S

> In baby yoga I find the singing really uplifting. I have learnt lots of new songs and whenever my baby is tearful I sing one of the songs and it really helps to change her mood.
> — Mary T

> What I like about baby yoga is that it's good for my well-being too. It includes lots of relaxing breaths and stretches to help me feel less stressed.
> — Jenny S

CHECKLIST OF WHAT WE'VE COVERED

In this chapter we've looked at:

♡ Baby Yoga and its benefits

♡ Having fun with some Baby Yoga exercises to help bring some relief from discomfort and to lift the spirits

♡ Consider joining a baby group so that you can meet and talk to other parents and carers, have some fun and learn more exercises.

BABY COLIC HELP

CHAPTER SIX
CRANIOSACRAL THERAPY

In this chapter we're going to look at craniosacral therapy as a treatment which can be very helpful for babies, especially for those who are crying a lot or showing colicky symptoms.

As a practising craniosacral therapist, I'm really passionate about cranioSacral therapy (CST)! It's a powerful balancing and healing treatment suitable for all ages. With its roots in osteopathy, it was developed into a unique treatment by John Upledger in the 1970s. It's a gentle, non-invasive, hands-on treatment, which works with the body's rhythms to activate the natural capacity for healing to correct imbalances within the craniosacral system.

THE CRANIOSACRAL SYSTEM

The craniosacral system has been in place since an early stage of our evolution. It comprises the bones of the skull (cranium and mandible), the spine, the sacrum and tailbone (coccyx), plus the membranes and fluid that surround and protect the brain and spinal cord, along with the related connective tissue.

Its function is to help maintain a healthy environment for the central nervous system (CNS) to function efficiently, thus influencing a variety of bodily functions.

WHY MIGHT YOUR BABY BENEFIT FROM CRANIOSACRAL THERAPY?

Childbirth can sometimes be complicated and babies can face a number of stressful challenges on their journey into this world. Some evidence suggests that a high percentage of all newborn babies may still hold a degree of birth stress afterwards.

The bones of the head are separate moving parts, wonderfully designed by nature to move and adjust as the baby travels through the birth canal. Babies' heads are designed to be flexible and strong enough to push their way out under pressure. However, CST therapists believe that problems can occur when cranial bones get twisted or compressed, and then stay out of shape.

This can sometimes happen after a baby has experienced:

- A forceps delivery
- A ventouse (vacuum) extraction
- A prolonged or traumatic birth.

Similar problems can happen within the spinal column, with pressure during birth causing a degree of twisting and slight misalignment. CST therapists believe that this could result in disturbance to the nerves at the back of the neck, for example those responsible for relaxing and tensing muscles, leaving your baby feeling very uncomfortable and unsettled.

Misalignment could have an impact on nerves of the central nervous system that branch out from the spine, transmitting essential messages to and from the whole body. These nerves require good skeletal alignment and space to function properly.

COLICKY SYMPTOMS

Bearing all this in mind, you can see how it's possible that your baby could be feeling discomfort in the gut and trying to communicate this through crying and through body language. Minor misalignment could interfere with messages efficiently reaching the digestive system, resulting in your baby experiencing colicky symptoms.

HOW DOES CRANIOSACRAL THERAPY WORK?

When your baby is feeling safe, loved and relaxed, they may be more able to communicate their areas of tensions. When these tensions are released and balanced, the baby is more likely to wholly relax into life. A sensitive, compassionate therapist will find those areas in need of adjustment and provide an opportunity for balancing to occur.

Gentle hands-on techniques facilitate the unwinding of areas of compression and misalignment, encouraging the release of stress and associated emotions. Your baby's body can then start to soften and relax. With pressure and tension gone, necessary space in the brain and body could return; room is freed for natural growth and functioning, and your baby's health and wellbeing could be much improved.

It's also possible that craniosacral therapy could help to release residual tension around the stomach and colon. It could also aid the stretching and relaxing of the Psoas muscles in the hips, which may be tight after months of your baby being in a flexed, foetal position in the womb.

WHEN IS IT BEST FOR YOUR BABY TO HAVE A CST TREATMENT?

Anecdotal evidence suggests that many newborn babies could benefit from craniosacral treatment within two weeks of birth – ideally in the first few days. This could help prevent many subsequent problems in childhood and adulthood, including some ear problems, developmental problems, headaches, neck pain and spinal disorders.

It's worth considering taking your baby to be checked over by a CST therapist in order to give them a good start in life. On average, at least three treatments are required; however differences may be noticeable after just one treatment. After a difficult delivery, and for premature babies, more treatments may be needed and it may take a few sessions before any significant changes are noticed. Also, it's good to know that it's never too late to make a difference – older children and even adults can benefit from CST.

HERE ARE SOME COMMENTS FROM MUMS AFTER THEIR BABIES HAD RECEIVED CRANIOSACRAL TREATMENT

> I had a traumatic time; there was a failed ventouse delivery, followed by an emergency forceps delivery. Afterwards my baby would cry for no apparent reason and she certainly didn't like her head being touched. I just felt there was something wrong. After a craniosacral treatment she was much calmer, less tearful and happier to be touched. I felt differently about her and we were closer.
> — *Denise M.*

> I had a very long labour; they found the cord had circled my baby's neck and it ended up being a ventouse delivery. Afterwards my baby was very unhappy; she didn't like being bathed or her neck being touched. I felt so stressed after my labour experiences and so upset to see her so unhappy. It was fantastic – after one treatment she was happier and more trusting and she started to like baths!
> — *Tracey Y.*

> Now that I have a happier baby I feel more relaxed in myself and I feel more able to go out and visit people with my baby. The whole family enjoy him so much more and I now have time to spend more time with my other children.
> — *Sara T.*

CHECKLIST OF WHAT WE'VE COVERED

In this chapter we've looked at:

- ♥ The craniosacral system

- ♥ Why your baby might benefit from CST

- ♥ How craniosacral therapy works

- ♥ When it's best for your baby to have a treatment.

BABY COLIC HELP

CHAPTER SEVEN
WHAT YOU CAN DO FOR YOU

This chapter discusses some of the natural thoughts and feelings you could be experiencing right now, and explores ways in which you can support yourself during stressful times.

YOU ARE IMPORTANT

Right from the beginning of the parenting journey it's good to remind yourself frequently that you are a valued person who has taken on the responsible role of being a parent. Being a mum will naturally take up a lot of your time and energy, and, being the mum of a colicky baby, will demand even more from you.

When we feel tired and exhausted, we may use whatever energy we can muster to try to satisfy the needs of our baby and other loved ones to the extent of leaving ourselves out. When this becomes a daily habit we can start to feel disconnected and out of touch with our own feelings, needs and individual identity.

It's healthier for everyone, and especially important for your long-term wellbeing, if you can slip some time into your day when you reconnect again. Just saying 'hi' to yourself from time to time will help to keep your energy levels topped up and your spirit fresh.

DEALING WITH EMOTIONS

Do you sometimes feel a jumble of emotions and just don't know how to find some peace? We often approach parenting with a mixture of our own personal feelings and beliefs, observations, theoretical knowledge and some unique emotional memories left over from our childhood. Sometimes we are aware of them, sometimes not. Having a baby is an incredibly profound experience; it's no wonder that you could be faced with a whole mixture of emotions, some of which could be quite unsettling.

We can have great expectations of how we would like things to be. Perhaps the pregnancy, birth, your baby's health or your own health didn't match up to those hopes and desires. Maybe your baby isn't feeding or sleeping well and you and those around you are feeling stressed and exhausted. When you're low in energy your emotions can get heightened and feel much worse: it could seem that everyone else's babies are perfect, that you're doing something wrong and that you're missing out somehow.

HERE ARE SOME COMMENTS FROM MUMS I'VE TALKED TO WHO HAVE EXPERIENCED SIMILAR FEELINGS.

> Nothing I do seems to work. I just don't feel confident about anything.
> — Tara N.

> I feel guilty about being happy when my baby is so unhappy.
> — Yvonne C.

> This was not how it was supposed to be. It's so disappointing!
> — Gemma B.

Whatever your emotions may be – extreme tiredness, anger, frustration, sadness, impatience, disillusionment – feeling them doesn't mean you're a bad parent. Your feelings are entirely natural, and it's better to acknowledge and express them rather than try to repress them. Holding in your negative feelings will not help you in any way; eventually they may cause so much more stress and bad feeling that they could end up affecting your health, and are certain to affect others around you.

MANAGING STRESS

There's no substitute for experience to teach us about parenting, and learning how to manage our own stress is a vital part of the process. Here are some suggestions for ways to help you to relax and recharge.

- **BREATHE DEEPLY**
  Taking several deep breaths will calm you, relaxing your body and helping you to think more clearly. Try sighing the breath out deeply, really feeling yourself letting go of stress and tension.

- **TALK TO SOMEONE**
  Talk to your partner, a family member, friend, counsellor or health professional. Sharing your feelings and identifying your needs with someone you're comfortable with may help you feel better. It's so important that your thoughts and feelings are acknowledged, expressed, and heard; repressing your feelings could eventually affect your health and wellbeing. By sharing your thoughts and feelings you may see a new perspective on your situation and find ways to move forward positively.

WHAT YOU CAN DO FOR YOU

♥ **WRITE YOUR FEELINGS DOWN**
Try writing down your thoughts and feelings every day; it can really help you to detach from them. In releasing them onto paper, you can view them more objectively and maybe become aware of new solutions.

♥ **ESSENTIAL OILS**
Chamomile and lavender oils are very relaxing and can help promote sleep (both are considered safe when breast freeding). Try adding a few drops to your bath. Geranium can be good for balancing hormones but, if breast feeding, just use it in a vaporiser or in a fresh air spray / spritzer. Check the usage with a professional.

♥ **TIME OUT AND FUN**
Ask for or accept help when it's offered and take some time out for yourself to unwind. Try listening to relaxing music, meditating, having a lovely bath or meeting up with a friend and having some well-deserved fun time.

♥ **LIST 10 THINGS FOR YOU**
Think of ten or more things you would love to do for ' you' and make a point of doing them. They don't have to be big things. Anything that gives you pleasure can go on your list; for example, paint your nails, have a walk on your own, read a page of your book. Try doing at least one small thing a day, and maybe something bigger once a week. This could make a big difference to how you feel.

♥ **DO LESS AND REST MORE**
In the early days with your new baby, don't expect to carry on as usual. You're very important, and your well-being is a priority, so you need to take whatever time you can to unwind and recharge. When your baby

sleeps, why don't you rest as well? This is a good time to talk to yourself sensibly and let yourself off the housework or other jobs you feel you should be doing. Take the 'should' away! If you have someone who could take over for a bit, why not let them? Not all the responsibility has to fall on your shoulders; you don't have to be super-mum all the time!

♥ HAVE SOME RELAXING HEALING THERAPY

Try some healing therapies to help you to relax and unwind, and to cope better with the ups and downs of it all. For example massage, aromatherapy, reflexology, craniosacral therapy (yes it's for adults too) and Pure Spiritual Healing can all help to balance and revitalise you.

♥ JOIN A PARENT AND BABY GROUP

Why not see what groups might be available in your area? Baby massage and baby yoga classes are particularly good for meeting other parents going through similar experiences, learning valuable techniques to help yourself and your baby, and having some fun with your baby. Ask your Health Visitor about groups in your area, and check the local papers, magazines and websites.

SUPPLEMENTS FOR MUM

It's worth thinking about taking nutritional supplements during this demanding time to help maintain your good health and well-being. It's important to support your body nutritionally, especially if you're breast-feeding and have a colicky baby. Stress and lack of sleep can deplete your body's natural reserves, and new mothers often can feel quite run down.

Always follow the recommended dosages.

♥ IRON

Iron is essential for preventing anaemia, which can lead to weakness, fatigue and increased risk of infection. If you have experienced heavy bleeding, have been feeling breathless, extremely tired or lightheaded, and your nail beds look pale, it's worth asking your GP for a blood test to check your iron levels. If an iron supplement is necessary, take a good quality one that is easily absorbed either in tablet or liquid form. If it's combined with Vitamin C, this will help absorption.

♥ B COMPLEX VITAMINS

Prolonged stress can affect your body and mind; by taking B vitamins you could help to support and strengthen your adrenal glands, nervous system and immune system, as well as helping to improve your energy and mood.

♥ MULTIVITAMINS

If you take a multivitamin supplement, one specifically formulated for pregnant or breast-feeding mothers could help you to stay well and give you more energy.

♥ ESSENTIAL FATTY ACIDS

The essential fatty acid Omega-3 is necessary for brain function and the balance of the autoimmune system. It's been suggested that supplementing an Omega-3 deficient diet could be helpful for your well-being as well as preventing allergies, colic and skin problems.

♥ MAGNESIUM

Prolonged stress could lead you to become deficient in magnesium. The more stressed you are, the greater the possibility of deficiency. Fatigue, muscle tension, spasms, twitching, irritability, hypersensitivity, tension headaches and having trouble falling asleep are all possible signs that your magnesium levels could be low.

NATURAL REMEDIES

You may like to know about some other alternative ways to help yourself. Here are some further suggestions.

(Check with a professional about how to use these remedies.)

HERBAL SUPPLEMENTS

Some herbs have been used for many years to increase milk production, with fenugreek, blessed thistle and red raspberry being among the most popular. None of these herbal remedies have been proven scientifically to increase milk supply, but mums have used them for hundreds if not thousands of years.

Other herbs that are considered safe are peppermint, red bush, chamomile and rosehip. These herbs can be infused in hot water to make therapeutic teas to sip throughout the day.

BACH FLOWER ESSENCES

These remedies are made from flower extracts that are believed to have a positive effect on emotional imbalances and moods such as: fear, depression, lack of self-confidence, stress and worrying.

Bach Night Rescue Remedy is an alcohol-free combination of relaxing and calming Bach Flower Essences to calm emotions, reduce anxiety or stress and improve sleep.

In addition, bottle brush (Australian Bush Remedy) is purported to strong healing qualities. It is considered to be good for: healing the emotions, reducing fibrocystic lumps found in the breast and for improving bonding feelings between you and your baby.

HOMEOPATHY

Many people find homeopathic remedies helpful. Again, ask a professional before using homeopathic remedies.

- Mag phos 6c – for colic, can be taken by baby or by mother if breastfeeding
- Pulsatilla – to be taken by mum when the milk comes in, to help prevent the baby blues
- Calc carb 6c – for galactorrhea (too much milk)
- Bell 6c – for mastitis (red and throbbing breast)
- Bryonia 6c – when the breast is white, hard and stony.

EATING WELL

Try not to skip meals; it's important to keep your energy levels up with good, nutritional food at regular intervals.

Breakfast is important; it helps to stimulate your metabolism, giving you good level of energy for your day. Eat highly nutritious foods, for example oatmeal with fruit, wholegrain cereals, wholegrain breads, yoghurt, eggs and yeast spread (which contains important B vitamins). There are many alternatives if you are on a wheat or gluten free diet.

NUTRITIONAL FOODS AND SNACKS

Try foods which have a low GI (Glycemic Index, which measures the rise of your blood sugar levels after eating them). These are slowly digesting foods that will help you to sustain your energy levels throughout your busy day, such as:

- Oats – oatcakes
- Rye – rye crackers or rye breads
- Nuts – almonds, cashews, walnuts

- Avocados
- Seeds – pumpkin and sunflower
- Sweet potatoes
- Brown rice
- Yogurt – cow, goat or soya
- Natural unsugared muesli.

HEALTHY SNACK SUGGESTIONS

- Sandwiches – Salad, choice of cheese, marmite, hummus, fish, egg, tahini, avocados, sproutings (alfalfa or broccoli), seed spreads or cold meats.
- Oatcakes and a savoury topping of your choice
- Vegetable, miso or bean soup
- Yoghurts or fromage frais
- Nuts & seeds or nut / seed spreads e.g. almond or cashew
- Fresh fruit
- Milky drinks (made with cow, goat, soya, rice or oat milk)
- Juices – made from freshly juiced vegetables and fruit of your choice
- Smoothies made with fresh fruit and yoghurt or icecream.

SUPERFOODS FOR MUM

IRON-RICH FOODS
These include almonds, which are particularly good when breastfeeding, high quality animal or non-animal protein, and sesame seeds.

BLUEBERRIES AND OTHER BERRY FRUITS
The fruit and juice are rich in antioxidants and full of vitamins, minerals and carbohydrates for energy. Try to have at least two servings a day.

WHAT YOU CAN DO FOR YOU

- **BROWN RICE**
  This provides wholegrain carbohydrate for energy, nutrients and valuable fibre.

- **LEAFY GREEN VEGETABLES**
  Spinach, Swiss chard and broccoli (although avoid the broccoli if you're breast feeding – it could create wind) are good sources of non-dairy calcium, and contain Vitamin C and Iron. Green vegetables are filled with heart-healthy antioxidants.

- **WHOLE-WHEAT BREAD** (avoid if you're intolerant)
  This contains folic acid, which is crucial in pregnancy and for your baby's development, along with healthy fibre and iron for mum.

- **SALMON AND OTHER OILY FISH**
  These contain essential fatty acids (EFAs), which are important for maintaining good brain functioning, including memory and concentration, and for balancing moods.
  However these benefits are balanced by a small risk of undesirable levels of mercury, so the NHS and the American Food & Drug Administration (FDA) and Environmental Protection Agency (EPA) recommend sticking to 12 ounces or two average servings a week.

- **FLAX OIL**
  Contains essential Omega-3 and is good for brain function and for helping to balance mood and hormones.

- **WHEATGRASS**
  This is packed with vitamins, minerals, anti-oxidants, chlorophyll, live enzymes, amino-acids and fatty acids.

- **SPIRULINA**
  This blue-green algae contains easily digested protein, vitamins, anti-oxidants, minerals, chlorophyll, essential fatty acids and B vitamins – some authorities say it's especially high in B12, but this is debatable as others disagree!

- **SUNFLOWER AND PUMPKIN SEEDS**
  These seeds provide a variety of vitamins and minerals, including iron, calcium and magnesium.

- **SPROUTING SEEDS AND NUTS**
  Once sprouted, seeds and nuts can be up to 15 times more nutritional and are easier to digest. Alfalfa seeds, hemp seeds, mung beans, adzuki beans, wheatgrass seeds, chickpeas and almonds all sprout well.

CHECKLIST OF WHAT WE'VE COVERED

In this chapter we've looked at:

♡   Dealing with emotions

♡   Managing stress

♡   Supplements for mum

♡   Natural remedies

♡   Eating well

♡   Superfoods for mum.

BABY COLIC HELP

CHAPTER EIGHT
BABY BLUES AND POST-NATAL DEPRESSION

In this chapter we'll be looking at symptoms of Post-Natal Depression and Baby Blues and offering suggestions to help and support you at this time.

It's completely normal to feel down soon after having your baby. Many mothers experience the 'baby blues' when the milk comes in, about three days after giving birth, due to hormonal changes. However, the baby blues naturally lift in a few days, so if you're still feeling down after several weeks it's possible that you may still be feeling low because of your circumstances, or you may have post natal depression (PND). In either case you need to get some help.

If you think you may be suffering with post-natal depression, it's important to know that you're not alone. PND is manageable and curable, and there's a lot of understanding and support available to help you to overcome it.

You need to be honest with yourself about how you're feeling. Thoughts and emotions, such as guilt, embarrassment, a feeling of inadequacy, or fear that you're a 'bad mum', could be preventing you from acknowledging that you might have PND, and getting in the way of your taking positive steps to do something about it. Try to find the courage to face it and speak up about it so that it doesn't affect you and your loved ones.

Media and cultural conditioning may lead us to believe that if we don't have the perfect relationship, home-life and birth and fall instantly in love with our babies from day one, we're somehow a failure. But it's time to be real: life is a mixture of challenges and joys and at this stage you're being faced with a challenge that can help you to grow as a person. It's possible that you're not concerned about your general circumstances yet still feel overwhelmed and down. Or perhaps you're aware of just not feeling right in yourself since your baby's birth. It's important to be kind to yourself at this time, and to remind yourself that there is nothing to be ashamed of: statistics show that around one in five mums suffer from some degree of post natal depression.

We're going to look now at some possible symptoms, to help you to decide whether you do have post-natal depression; then we'll look at some of the causes, followed by some ways to help you to feel more positive.

SYMPTOMS OF PND

Do you have any of the following symptoms?

- Persistent low mood, particularly worse first thing in the morning; do you not really enjoy anything and have a lack of interest in yourself and your baby?
- Emotional numbness, feeling as if your baby is not really yours
- Strong feelings of not being able to cope
- Extreme mood swings
- Frequently tearful
- Anger or irritability
- Fear and anxiety most of the time; anxious or obsessive about cleanliness or your baby's health, welfare and safety
- Horrible and distressing thoughts about yourself and your baby; suicidal thoughts

If you've answered 'yes' to any of these questions then it's possible that you have some degree of post natal depression. Be kind to yourself and acknowledge that you need help so you can take positive steps forward to resolve it. Start by seeking professional help as soon as you can.

POSSIBLE CAUSES OF POST-NATAL DEPRESSION

Let's look now at some of the possible causes of PND.

- A history of depression.
- Hormonal changes
- Stresses and anxieties
- A traumatic birthing experience
- Sleep deprivation
- Anaemia.

Whatever the reasons for your feeling low, it's good to see that the best thing you can do for yourself and your baby is to start opening up, talking about it with someone you feel comfortable with, and thinking about how you can put positive things in place to help to recharge you.

In addition to speaking to your GP or Health Visitor why not try some of the following suggestions for Post-Natal Baby Blues.

POST- NATAL DEPRESSION HELPLINE

www.pndsupport.co.uk

SUGGESTIONS FOR HELPING POST-NATAL BABY BLUES OR WHEN YOU'RE FEELING LOW:

- **ACKNOWLEDGE HOW YOU FEEL – AND TALK TO SOMEONE**
  Try to find the courage to talk to someone you feel safe with: your partner, a good friend, relative, health visitor or your doctor. Sometimes just talking will help reduce some of your anxiety. It's important you get the help and support you need during this time.

- **PRACTICAL ISSUES**
  Look for any independent advice you might need regarding financial worries, help with childcare, etc. For example you might go to the Citizens Advice Bureau or your local Job Centre, and also look for online help.

- **COUNSELLING AND OTHER TALKING THERAPIES**
  Talking to a counsellor is a confidential and safe way to air

thoughts and feelings. If you're dealing with birth trauma, counselling could help you to 'off load' and work through some of your thoughts and feelings. See this as taking an active step towards learning from your experiences and moving on with a healthier mind. Ask your doctor for help with finding a suitable counsellor.

♡ NATURAL REMEDIES

Speak with a Herbalist, Homeopath, Naturopath or Nutritionist about what natural remedies and supplements are recommended for balancing hormones, calming and strengthening nerves and balancing emotions.

♡ ABDOMINAL BREATHING

Breathing deeply, down into your abdomen, is a simple and effective way of helping you to keep your nervous system strong, to think more calmly and clearly, give yourself more energy and be more mindful. Everyone can benefit from consciously breathing fully, especially during times of stress or worry. Take in a deep breath through the nose, feeling your lungs expanding fully right down to the bottom of the ribcage. Allow your belly to expand a little as you do this. Then breathe out deeply through the mouth with a slow gentle sigh, and let your belly naturally deflate. Repeat three times. Do this several times a day, or whenever you feel you need to.

♡ VISUALISATION

This visualisation technique can help you if you're feeling angry, anxious or low. Sit or lie down comfortably, then take a couple of deep breaths. Imagine your emotions forming a ball of energy attached to a big helium balloon, which then floats up and out of your body. If you'd like to explore visualisation techniques further, you might like to buy a guided relaxation CD (see FURTHER RESOURCES).

♥ **REST WHEN YOU CAN**
When your baby sleeps, why don't you take the opportunity to have a rest? This is a good time to talk to yourself sensibly and let yourself off the housework and other chores – it's more important that you take the time to unwind and recharge. If you find that you're too tired to just switch off, don't worry: you can do some deep abdominal breathing, listen to relaxing music or to a guided relaxation CD, or just stretch out somewhere and do nothing.

♥ **GET REGULAR EXERCISE AND BE IN THE PRESENCE OF NATURE**
Make sure you get out at least once a day and, if possible, walk where you can make some contact with nature. Go to the park and stand by a tree or lovely plant, or anywhere that feels good to you. Being outside in the fresh air with natural daylight or sunlight lifts the spirits. Nature has an uplifting energy which we can all benefit from. Just being by water, under a tree or listening to bird song can help us to feel more balanced and uplifted.

♥ **JOIN AN EXERCISE CLASS**
Gentle exercise classes like Yoga, Tai Chi or, if you prefer, something more energetic, are all good to help you to get out, balance your body and mind and lift your spirits. If you're unable or prefer not to go to a class, watch a DVD or get some books to guide you through some restorative exercises.

♥ JOIN A PARENT AND BABY GROUP

Meeting and talking with other parents (they'll be having all sorts of feelings too) will enable you to feel less isolated, learn bonding techniques and have some fun. It will get you out of the house and lift your spirits. Baby Massage or Baby Yoga classes are excellent for helping you to relax and learn to connect with your baby.

♥ HAVE SOME HEALING THERAPY

Be kind to yourself. Consider having some healing therapy. It can really help you to relax, balance, recharge and feel less frazzled! It can help you to feel more able to cope with the ups and downs of it all. It could also help you with resolving any issue around the birth, or with any other issue that's concerning you. Pure Spiritual Healing, Massage, Reflexology, CranioSacral Therapy, Aromatherapy and Acupuncture are all very effective therapies that may help you in many ways.

♥ ASK FOR AND ACCEPT HELP

If someone you trust offers to help you, why not accept it? The responsibility of parenting doesn't have to fall heavily on your shoulders. Why not allow yourself a break to do whatever you feel like doing, including just resting?

♥ BOOKS

There are some great baby books and self-help books available for sale and from the library; you could find a great deal of information and support from them.

♥ LEARN TO MEDITATE

Meditation is a wonderful, life-enhancing practice to bring into your life. Meditation could help you to connect to an inner resource that will bring more peace, wisdom and well-being into your life.

♡ **LEARN TO LISTEN TO YOUR INTUITION**
Your inner knowing can be a friend and guide through all challenging times. Intuitive guidance has a peaceful essence. It feels like a deep knowing about something. Sometimes it's hard to explain how you know; you just do. It's seldom a negative thought and often comes through in a peaceful moment, quick as a flash. It's good to learn to trust this guidance.

Throughout this difficult time it's important to keep sight of the 'light at the end of the tunnel'. This challenging period will end, and you'll have found out just how resilient you can be under pressure. Every challenging experience in life gives us an opportunity to grow and to learn more about ourselves and others. It helps us to develop more inner strength and it certainly helps us to be more compassionate towards others. You're never truly alone, even if it feels like it. You can ask for help inwardly as well as outwardly and your intuition will help and guide you.

CHECKLIST OF WHAT WE'VE COVERED

In this chapter we've looked at:

♡ Baby Blues and Post-Natal Depression

♡ Talk to someone. If you think you might have PND, or are not sure, find the courage to talk to someone you feel safe with

♡ Ways to help you with Baby Blues and for when you're feeling low.

BABY COLIC HELP

CHAPTER NINE
MORE FOR DADS

In this chapter we're looking at different aspects of parenting from a father's point of view, with suggestions of ways for you, the father, to deal with any challenges.

While there are no hard and fast gender roles with regard to parenting, it's fair to say that mothers and fathers display tendencies towards different approaches. It may be useful for you to identify some of the differences in approach that naturally occur, especially in the early stages of parenting. And, if you're a single dad, it may also be useful for you to identify your areas of strength as well as the areas where you might welcome extra back-up due to your circumstances.

DIFFERENT ISN'T BAD, JUST DIFFERENT

Research shows that men can nurture as well as women can; good parenting is down to practice. However, men and women tend to favour different ways of interacting with a baby. For example:

- Men tend to enjoy being more physical and energetic, playing noisy rough and tumble games.

- Women tend to deal more with the baby's emotional needs, for example having quiet times, and being the primary feeder and nurturer; they also tend to cover the social needs, such as meeting up with other mums and babies, joining parent and baby groups, and attending clinics.

Of course, there are no hard and fast divisions; your baby needs both kinds of input and will respond differently to each parent. And also, roles can be shared with others, according to what works for you both as a couple, or you as a single parent.

YOU WEREN'T EXPECTING TO FEEL THIS WAY

In the early days, mum and baby become extremely preoccupied with getting acquainted. Feeling the dynamics of your relationship change, you now may not be sure where you fit in. You may be concerned that your partner doesn't love you as much any more. You may feel pressure to be the 'strong man', when the truth is that you haven't slept in days and feel physically and mentally exhausted and possibly a little lost.

However, it's also possible that you could be misinterpreting how your partner is really feeling about you and also her own parenting role at this time; she could be finding it just as hard to adjust to the radical change as you are!

Whatever the case, it's likely that the focus of attention is naturally more centred on mum and baby, and you may be feeling that your needs and feelings are being overlooked. Possibly you're feeling the weight of the financial and emotional responsibilities of parenthood, even feeling a little bit overwhelmed by it.

Maybe it all didn't seem that real until the moment actually arrived, and arrive it did in a rather dramatic and profound fashion! You've seen this miracle unfolding in front of your eyes, and now you're trying to be actively supportive while actually feeling quite daunted and possibly a little superfluous.

It's important that you acknowledge and accept how you feel, realise that you are not alone, and understand that there is no need to feel guilty or ashamed of your feelings or concerns. Do your best to get involved in your little baby's care as much as possible; the more you experience you gain, the more you will relax into your parenting role, and it won't be long before your baby's unconditional love will warm your heart.

However, if your feelings continue to trouble you over a period of time, raise your concerns with somebody else, whether a professional or just someone you trust and feel comfortable with.

FINDING IT HARD TO BOND

It's fair to say that many dads find it difficult to bond with their newborn baby straight away. It's normal to experience a mixture of emotions. Trying to bond with your baby while he or she is suffering from colicky symptoms is not always easy: lots of patience is needed at this time – and, don't forget, it will not last for ever! Your baby needs your love and support a great deal.

SOME SUGGESTIONS TO HELP WITH BONDING

- **CUDDLES!**
  Simple but wonderful, just cuddling your baby will help to reassure both you that you matter to each other. Cuddling is a natural way to give and receive affection. It also encourages the release of the 'feel-good' hormone oxytocin in both of you, which helps with the bonding process.

- **TIME TOGETHER**
  Bath your baby, go out and about together, sit with your baby for a while or try some baby massage. Baby massage will help to bring you closer together in a relaxed and loving way; you'd be amazed at how wonderful you could feel afterwards. (See Chapter Four: IN YOUR LOVING HANDS).

- **PLAYTIME**
  Have some fun together, just enjoying each other's company! Sit and talk to your baby – they will love to hear your voice. Try some baby yoga exercises, easy movements that you can combine with swings and lifts. This time together can greatly help you bond further while having fun along the way. (See Chapter Five: BABY YOGA).

- **JUMP IN**
  Get involved in the practicalities of baby care. Share

some of the tasks, such as nappy changing, feeding, and dressing your baby. This would greatly help your partner, giving her some 'baby-free' time out, as well as deepening your relationship with your baby.

FEELING DOWN

Some research suggests that around 4% of men experience post-natal blues. Odd as it may sound, you could feel simultaneously empowered and disempowered: empowered because you have this new love, and disempowered because you're feeling vulnerable about your being responsible for this new being.

Canadian researcher Anne Storey found that new fathers' testosterone levels drop radically, by up to one third, after childbirth. Testosterone affects energy and mood, so this can result in feeling a little down. These lowered hormone levels, however, can also be beneficial, increasing your tolerance and helping you to feel calmer, which all helps with the bonding process.

Other stresses and anxieties could also contribute to the dampening of your feelings. Perhaps you're feeling low because of the number of changes you are having to make to your lifestyle, as well as feeling the weight of the responsibility of being a provider and supporter. You're not alone with these thoughts; it's natural to have them. You can't really appreciate what it's like having a baby to care for until it happens, and there is bound to be a transition time where all sorts of concerns arise. It's important to remember that they will resolve in time. However, it is best to talk about them now if they are getting you down.

JEALOUSY AND RESENTMENT

It's not uncommon for men to find it difficult to adjust to the arrival of a baby and the radical changes this brings. The difficulties are increased if there's the possibility that you're misinterpreting how your partner is really feeling about you at this time when she is trying, like you, to adjust to the radical changes that she is experiencing.

DO YOU FEEL...

- That you're not bonding with your baby as well as your partner is
- Ignored most of the time
- Angry – about the time that your partner is spending with the baby
- Frustrated – because you're not able to do all the things you used to do before you had the baby
- Unsure about what you're doing most of the time?

ACKNOWLEDGE HOW YOU ARE FEELING

It's good to be honest with yourself and acknowledge how you are feeling right now. You don't have to be ashamed about these feelings – they are not uncommon. But, even though you wouldn't wish them to, they could be negatively affecting your behaviour towards your baby and your partner, so it's a good idea to address them.

Try not to hide away and bury your feelings of jealousy and resentment; this decision could be dis-empowering and destructive. Left unaddressed, they can damage your relationship and your experience of fatherhood.

Try to be as open as you can and share your thoughts clearly and honestly with your partner, not in a shaming or blaming way, but just to air them. If you're reluctant to share these thoughts with your partner, perhaps not wishing to burden her, or for some other good reason, then try writing your feelings down. This gives you a way to express them and also to look at them more clearly and objectively.

Then find a trusted friend, family member, counsellor or doctor to talk them over with. It's important that your feelings are acknowledged and heard in some way.

CONSTANT CRYING

Some research suggests that hearing the sound of a baby crying can trigger unique emotional responses in us. Within 100 milliseconds, about as long as it takes to blink, parts of our brain react. Primitive parts of the brain connected to fight or flight responses cause us to feel alert and ready to respond and, if we are unable to help, we can feel quite disturbed or irritated.

The more time you spend getting to know your baby, the better you will understand the different types of crying — for example being hungry, or tired, or needing a nappy change — and the easier it will be to cope with it. All your baby is trying to do is communicate in the only way they know.

Try taking some deep breaths (abdominal breaths), when you feel yourself getting uptight and irritated or alarmed by the crying. This will help you to feel calmer and more clear headed and better able to deal with the situation at hand.

HOW TO DO ABDOMINAL BREATHING

Take a deep breath in through the nose, feeling your lungs expanding fully, right down to the bottom of the ribcage. Allow your stomach to expand a little as you do this. Then breathe out deeply through the mouth with a slow, gentle sigh, and let your stomach naturally deflate. Repeat for two or three breaths, whenever you need to.

LOVEMAKING CHANGES

The lack of physical intimacy could be another reason for feeling down. You may feel that intimacy would help you to feel more involved, loved and needed – but your partner is not so keen. Maybe she is just too tired; she may be exhausted! There could be physical and hormonal reasons why intercourse could be unappealing, uncomfortable or even extremely painful for your partner right now. Or maybe she's just not feeling attractive and in the mood.

Be aware that your feelings could be heightened at the moment and you could be misunderstanding and possibly over-reacting to your partner's lack of interest. Try not to assume that she doesn't care about you, or that you're not important to her any more; these thoughts might be totally untrue and could be very destructive.

In the early stages your partner will be dealing with considerable hormonal and lifestyle changes and it's natural that there could be a difference in your sex drives at this point. Be aware, if your partner is not physically or emotionally ready, it's best not to push for it. Pressure is not an aphrodisiac! Remind yourself that this is just a stage of adjustment; it will pass and you will be loved and respected even more for your loving understanding.

You may be feeling frustrated and tense because you miss your usual levels of fulfilment derived from sexual interaction with your partner. This is more common than you might imagine; if it's happening to you, acknowledge your feelings and know that you're not the only one. I'm sure you can find ways to deal with those frustrations naturally for yourself!

HEIGHTENED FEELINGS

Be aware that pent-up sexual energy can charge up emotions and feelings and have a powerful influence over your rational thoughts. You may be convincing yourself that your partner is rejecting you, punishing you or just doesn't love you any more. Try not to let these fears take you over as truths. Do what you can to clear your energy and thoughts constructively as soon as possible.

It is also possible that your partner is being emotionally and physically quite needy at this time. Try not to think that you are doing something wrong. And don't fall into the trap of wanting to fix everything. Sometimes, women just want to express themselves and feel heard! Try to be there for her by listening and encouraging her the best you can. You'd be surprised how much closer your partner will then feel to you, and more likely to be ready for physical closeness sooner.

COUPLE CARE

Look after each other! This is a time for understanding and patience. There are many ways to give and receive love and affection, which, in the long run, could enhance your relationship even further. It's important for you both to plan some time together so that you can look after your relationship with each other.

While you'll naturally have different needs at this time, it's likely that you'd both benefit from having some adult time where possible. With a certain amount of flexibility, why not plan a date, a walk, a trip out – anything that feels right and can be managed child-free. Remind each other in little ways just how important you are to one another: little notes, flowers and presents all show how appreciated and loved you are. Being kind and respectful to each other will help to keep a flow of love and good feeling between you. This strengthening of your bond together can greatly help you in dealing with those inevitable challenges along the parenting journey. Cherish what you have.

WHEN ADVICE IS GIVEN TO YOU ON YOUR PARENTING

You and your partner may be finding that many people have different opinions on good parenting. You could be finding that current trends differ greatly from the ideas that were around for your parents, such as the best ways to settle your baby to sleep, whether to leave them to cry or not, and whether to use a dummy or not. However, those around you may have valuable experience and wisdom worth listening to and acting upon.

Their advice could be welcome and helpful – or could be causing tension between you and your partner. Perhaps you could both agree that, even though you're happy to listen to suggestions from your parents and other sources, such as other family members, midwives, health visitors, and books and the internet, you will discuss the advice given with each other first, before adopting any changes.

CHECKLIST FOR WHAT WE'VE COVERED

In this chapter we've looked at:

- ♡ Different approaches
- ♡ Relationship changes
- ♡ Bonding
- ♡ Feeling down
- ♡ Jealousy and resentment
- ♡ Constant crying
- ♡ Lovemaking changes
- ♡ Couple care
- ♡ Others' parenting advice.

BABY COLIC HELP

YOU ARE A COLIC HERO!

However challenging and exhausting this time is for you, just remember: it will pass! It will not last for ever, even if that's how it feels at the moment. This book's aim has been to get you through this demanding time. Use your intuition, try as many different ways to help yourself and your baby as you can, and have faith that this phase will end.

Once this time has passed and peace and harmony is restored, why not reflect back on your experiences? It's the hardest times that can teach us the most valuable lessons. See how you have survived the baby colic challenge and how you have become even stronger as a person because of it. Be aware of the areas where you have become more resilient and resourceful.

Adversity holds many gifts: the gifts of learning and growing, opening up to new ways of thinking and being, finding hidden depths within ourselves, and developing understanding and compassion for others.

Take heart. All that you do for your baby and yourself through love and kindness will reap many benefits. Dealing with colic is an intense experience. Be kind, and be proud of yourself, for you are a Colic Hero!

BABY COLIC HELP

APPENDIX

HEART TO HEART WITH YOUR BABY

In this appendix we're going to look at three meditation or visualisation practices that you may find helpful to do for both yourself and your baby.

For each of these three practices, I suggest you read through the instructions several times to familarise yourself with them before you have a go. You may find it helpful to record yourself reading them aloud, so you can just listen to the instructions as you do the practice.

HEART CONNECTION

To make sure you won't be disturbed, why don't you switch off the television and radio, and make sure the landline is on answer phone and your mobile is on silent? Before you find a quiet place to sit or lie down comfortably, take a minute just to loosen up your body. Do some gentle stretches in any way that feels right; you're more likely to be able to settle if you do this first. You may find covering yourself in a blanket helpful; it will keep you warm and will help to give your mind and body a signal that it's time to relax. If you're going to be sitting up, make sure that your back and legs are well supported. If you're going to lie down, you may want to support your neck and head with a cushion or towel. If lying with your legs straight out is uncomfortable, you could place a cushion under your knees or just bend them up instead.

Once you're settled, you may like to close your eyes, and take three deep, slow breaths, in through the nose and out through the mouth. These breaths will help to relax and nourish you.

Begin by bringing your awareness to your feet and ankles. Give them permission to let go of tension or discomfort.

Extend your awareness to your legs, your calves, knees and thighs; encourage them to let go, soften and relax.

Now bring your relaxation up to the hips and abdomen; release any tension and let it go. Feel your body letting any tension just melt away.

Bring your awareness up to the chest area and release any tightness or tension here; feel yourself letting go. Relax. Feel your chest opening and expanding, and relax.

Extend your relaxation to your shoulders and arms. If you like, try gently raising your shoulders up towards your ears, hold, then relax them down again.

Now gently relax your neck. If you like, move your head gently from side to side, then bring it back to the centre to rest. Let go and relax.

Feel that your whole body is warm, comfortable and relaxed.

Now bring your awareness to your heart centre, in the middle of your chest. Notice, from here, how you give and receive love. When there's a natural flow, you can feel wonderful. When there's tension, maybe due to fears, old hurts and pains, that flow can be affected and you can feel out of balance. Let go of that tension now, imagining it just melting away.

Now you can gently help that wonderful flow of love from your heart to nurture and nourish you and others. Imagine what it would be like if you could think of some source of pure loving light and energy, that is part of all life. This source can be imagined like the sun's rays. Feel these rays are beaming towards you. Now ask these rays of love to safely touch your heart centre; and as they do, be aware of how gentle and warm they feel. Whether you can feel them, or not, just know that they are there.

Imagine now that your whole chest area is filling up with this light and is feeling soft, warm and relaxed. This light is loving and healing. Now feel that loving light shining out from your chest centre and into the world. Imagine this light reaching your baby and your family, balancing and healing.

Take a few moments to feel this pure light pouring out from your heart centre. If at any time you find your mind wandering off, thinking of something else, just gently bring your awareness back to your heart centre again. This natural flow of light is always there; it's yours to enjoy and appreciate.

Now, in a short while, start to come out of your relaxation practice. When you're ready, take a couple of deep breaths, then move or stretch a little. If you feel the need to be more alert before getting up, rub your hands together, then rub your legs up and down. This will help to ground you.

As you get more familiar with this visualisation, you may like to enhance it by extending the light to other babies and parents and even further afield to all those in need.

TONGLEN

The next meditation is based on an ancient Buddhist practice called tonglen. It's a positive method for overcoming fear of suffering; it helps to dissolve tightness in our hearts and awakens the natural compassion that is inherent in all of us.

This practice could help you to deal with difficult bouts of baby colic when you feel distressed by your baby's pain and suffering.

When your baby is troubled, and you wish you could take their pain away, you can imagine that you could somehow breathe in their pain, breathing it into yourself with your in-breath. Imagine you could breathe all their pain and discomfort into your own loving heart; if you like, you could visualise it as a kind of dark vapour. Then, as you breathe out, feel that pain being transformed in your loving heart into healing love, relief and peace that you can send back out to your baby; if you like, visualise that as a lovely white or golden light. Repeat these transforming breaths until you feel more at ease.

You can also do this practice to help yourself if you are suffering in some way. Perhaps you're feeling sad, angry or afraid; or maybe you can't name the emotion precisely, but you can feel it as tightness in the stomach, or a sense of heaviness or darkness; or perhaps you're just not happy. The practice is to breathe in for all those countless others in the world feeling the same emotions as you, right now, and then, when you breathe out, send everyone, including yourself, love, relief and peace as a white or golden light.

A HEALING LIGHT PRACTICE

A Healing Light practice can also be done for yourself, your baby or anyone you want to help in some way – an animal, friend, relative, or anyone who is suffering in the world.

Think of or visualise who ever you want to direct the practice to. Imagine that they are surrounded in a healing bubble of light, and send them your loving thoughts and feelings. Be thankful for that wonderful loving resource you have inside you.

BABY COLIC HELP

FURTHER RESOURCES

BOOKS

Tracey Hogg with Melinda Blau	*The Baby Whisperer*
Etienne and Neeto Peirsman	*Craniosacral Therapy for Babies and Small children*
Mark Atkinson	*The Mind Body Bible*
Louise L Hay	*You Can Heal Your Life*
William Sears, M.D. & Martha Sears R.N.	*The Baby Book*
Mata Yogananda Mahasaya Dharma	*The Truth Eternal*
Mata Yogananda Mahasaya Dharma	*Gods in the Making*
Vimala McClure	*Infant Massage – A Handbook for Loving Parents*
Armin A Brott	*The New Father – A Guide to the First Year*
Jan de Vries	*Pregancy and Childbirth*
Pauline Carpenter and Anita Epples	*The Definitive Guide for Teaching Parents*
Francoise Barbira Freedman	*Baby Yoga*

WEBSITES

PARENT SUPPORT
www.cry-sis.org.uk
www.nhs.uk/parenting
www.nhs.uk/start4life

POST-NATAL DEPRESSION SUPPORT
www.pndsupport.co.uk
www.regenerativenutrition.com
www.patient.co.uk

BREAST FEEDING SUPPORT
www.breastfeedingnetwork.org.uk

SELF REALIZATION MEDITATION HEALING CENTRE
www.selfrealizationcentres.org

BABY COMMUNICATION
www.dunstanbaby.com

INFORMATION ON BABY COLIC, TREATMENTS AND COACHING SERVICES
www.babycolichelp.co.uk

INFORMATION ON NATURAL THERAPIES AND GUIDED RELAXATION CDS
www.true-nature.co.uk

Printed in Great Britain
by Amazon